"When I think (... are tw..

'Few are those who can see with their own ..., their own hearts.' —Albert Einstein

Al is one of those who could do this as a freshman in college, deciding where he could best pursue his dreams.

Secondly is the indigenous saying,

'The elders have visions and the youth have dreams.'

Looking back, the young Al Carius as a freshman in college actually possessed the visions of an elder and the dreams of the youth.

He went on to become one of the greatest mentors and coaches in America as he empowered the youth with the wisdom to follow their dreams and to see with their own eyes and feel with their own hearts."

—Billy Mills, *Tamakoce Te'hila (Loves His Country),* Oglala Lakota, Olympic Gold Medal, 10,000 Meters, Tokyo 1964

"So now you are about to read a loving and thoughtful volume about a man who could not be more revered, loved, admired, and respected by those he coached and influenced. . . . What's interesting though is, this book is NOT about his own achievements or his many personal accolades, acknowledgements, or awards. No, this book is about his athletes and the philosophy and wisdom behind his legacy as a coach, man, mentor, and friend."

—Chief Judge Kenneth L. Popejoy, 18th Judicial Circuit Court, DuPage County, Illinois North Central Assistant Coach 1982-93, Cross Country and Track & Field, Ranked 9th in the World in the Mile/1500meters, 1975

Cover photo: Weigel, Henz, and Dickerson
1993 NCAA Division III National Championships
Team and *Knowing*

Photo credit: Coach Frank Gramarosso

RUN FOR FUN AND PERSONAL BESTS

To MERICA,

God Bless,

Coach Al Carius

RUN FOR FUN and PERSONAL BESTS

A Recipe for Long-Term Growth and Success

THE STORY OF
The North Central College
Cross Country and Track & Field Teams

COACH AL CARIUS

LUMINARE PRESS
WWW.LUMINAREPRESS.COM

Run for Fun and Personal Bests: A Recipe for
Long-Term Growth and Success
Copyright © 2021 by Coach Al Carius

Printed in the United States of America

Luminare Press
442 Charnelton St.
Eugene, OR 97401
www.luminarepress.com

LCCN: 2021915449
ISBN: 978-1-64388-737-1

To Coach Ted Haydon,
who showed me the way

TABLE OF CONTENTS

"A Coach can influence more young people in one year than the average person will in a lifetime."

—Reverend Billy Graham

"It seems to me that the recipe to success and long-term growth and development—in sports and in life—is as follows. Know yourself. Know where you want to go. Let nothing external distract you. Surround yourself with supportive people—your team—sharing similar goals. Believe in who you are, and turn your faith into the 'knowing' to follow... your internal 'servo-mechanism.' This is the path to becoming the best you can be."

—Coach Al Carius

"Most of what I know about coaching I learned in Sunday School."

—Coach Al Carius

Foreword from a
North Central Assistant Coach,
Ken Popejoy

Coach Al Carius's credo: six simple, easy to understand words, "RUN FOR FUN AND PERSONAL BESTS."

In the late summer of 1982, my life was in the midst of a serious downturn of emotion, unrest, and upheaval. I needed a "safe place" to try to stop the spiral and stabilize my mark in this world. My future was clouded, uncertain, and without a plan.

So, I showed up in the cross country office of Al Carius at tiny North Central College in Naperville, Illinois, and asked him if I could come down from my law practice in Wheaton, Illinois two days a week and run with his team. I needed an unquestioning friend, and Al Carius had been a great one since we first met in 1966 when he was at North Central College and I arrived as a freshman at Glenbard West High School.

Al was a runner of national renown. An individual Illinois Mile State Champion, a multiple Big Ten cross country and track & field champion, an NCAA All American, and a University of Chicago Track Club member who was nationally ranked in the steeplechase. But with all of these running credentials and accomplishments, he had morphed from a great athlete into a great coach.

At the close of Al's running career and at the end of his educational pursuits, he chose North Central College to be the place to start his coaching tenure. Despite many offers and opportunities to coach at other institutions over the next 55+ years, Al never left!

This book is filled with the stories of Al's days at North Central College. What's interesting though is, this book is *NOT* about his own achievements or his many personal accolades, acknowledgements, or awards. No, this book is about his athletes and the philosophy and wisdom behind his legacy as a coach, man, mentor, and friend.

You will read stories about "the law of specificity," Lincoln Park, "the hill," Mr. Temperature, the Tasmanian Devil, "All set?... You bet!" and so many more. You'll hear tales of champion runners and championship teams, but you'll also hear that that wasn't the primary goal of Coach Al Carius. Yes, those were *all* wonderful accomplishments and achievements but they were *never* the primary focus of Al's coaching pursuits.

Some of Al's greatest words help to show what he focused on:

"Be comfortable and confident with who you are."

"Find the 'why' in your life."

"You have to find *your* passion and then compete with yourself to be the best that you can and to win for yourself and not worry about how you compare with anybody else."

"I am only a track coach not a philosopher, psychologist, psychiatrist, etc." (*NOT* true... He has been *all* of those over and over again to each and every one of us.)

"You really are the happiest person in the world if you can only know it at the time."

Al would also quote his favorite saying from Emerson: "The hardest thing is to be yourself in a world that is trying to make you into something you are not." He loved this. "It's powerful," he would say.

All of these and many more are timeless "Al-isms." Where or how did he develop these thoughts, his philosophies of a sort?

Al grew up in small Morton, Illinois. His parents owned a Dairy Queen and a theatre in town. Ice cream and a movie always has been a great day for Al. His father was so much more than just a dad. He showed Al how to be a Christian, how to work toward a goal, how to be humble in victory and gracious in defeat, how to be a positive person, how to be comfortable and confident in who and what you are. Ted Hayden, his coach from the University of Chicago Track Club, was a "father figure" and his coaching mentor. John Wooden, famed UCLA basketball coach, once said what Al learned… to "coach his athletes from the inside out… character, discipline, work ethic."

So now you are about to read a loving and thoughtful volume about a man who could *not* be more revered, loved, admired, and respected by those he coached and influenced. The names of his athletes and assistant coaches, and how he touched each of those lives as a role model, mentor, lifelong friend, and coach, will fill the pages to follow.

I eventually did stop the spiral and stabilized my life in those early 1980s, and I so enjoyed and treasured Al's words and friendship that I stuck around another 12 wonderful years as one of his assistant coaches. I'll leave you, the reader, to discover which of those stories and recollections will affect *you* the most. My heart and soul are filled with those that have made me into who and what I am today.

You could try to paraphrase Al's "credo"… "Be the very best that you can be and have fun doing it." Or, "Have fun and, as a result, you will be your best in that moment." But the paraphrasing or rewording just doesn't cut it. No, "RUN FOR FUN AND PERSONAL BESTS" says it all... How motivational, how powerful, how caring!

North Central College was a special kind of place in the years of Al Carius. Al Carius is a special kind of person who will live in the hearts and souls of all of us forever. *ENJOY!*

Chief Judge Kenneth L. Popejoy
18th Judicial Circuit Court
DuPage County, Illinois

North Central Assistant Coach 1982-93
Cross Country and Track & Field

Ranked 9th in the World in the Mile/1500 meters, 1975

Foreword from a
North Central Alumni Runner

Blink and you might miss tiny North Central College. Tucked amongst stately Victorian homes in the Chicago suburb of Naperville, Illinois, the college and its roughly 3,000 students go largely unnoticed by the streams of passing cars on nearby Washington Street and Ogden Avenue.

I'd visited a handful of other schools in the Midwest as part of my college search, but North Central was my first choice. There were a lot of reasons to like the little college. It was close to family and just outside one of the country's great, dynamic cities. The campus was compact, but scenic, and filled with turn-of-the-century archetypal "college" buildings. Its small, intimate classes assuaged my fear of feeling lost at a big university.

But the real reason I and so many others came to Naperville from across Illinois—and the country—was Al Carius. The architect of one of the most successful college athletic programs, in any sport, in any division, Al has been the face of North Central for over 50 years. Since he arrived on North Central's campus in the fall of 1966, his teams have accumulated 19 NCAA Division III National Championships in cross country, 12 in track and field, 48 College Conference of Illinois and Wisconsin (CCIW) Championships in cross country, including the last 45 in a row, 38 CCIW Championships in track & field, and hundreds of conference champions and All Americans. He was named NCAA Division III Men's "Coach of the Century" by his peers in 2000.

Why has North Central been so successful, both in terms of national championships and its longevity?

Part of it can be explained by the intricacies of NCAA Division III, which uniquely suits the program's "Run for Fun and Personal Bests" philosophy. Schools in Division III do not offer athletic scholarships, nor do their athletic programs generate revenue. The result is that NCAA Division III is composed of a motley crew of hundreds of small liberal arts colleges like North Central, research universities that put more emphasis on academics than athletics (think Carnegie Mellon or MIT), and the bulk of some large state university systems. Nearly every school in the University of Wisconsin system, outside of Milwaukee and Madison, and a large chunk of the State University of New York system, for example, are Division III schools. All have one thing in common: their student athletes compete for the love of the sport, not scholarship money.

This alone, though, does not explain North Central's dominance. Special training techniques? We ran a lot of miles, a lot of hills, and a lot of intervals, but not much has changed over the last five decades. Several other teams have modeled their training regimen after North Central's, with varying levels of success.

Something in the water? Al has actually been asked that on at least one occasion and, sadly, the answer is no.

The truth is, there is no one grand reason that explains the success and longevity of North Central College Cross Country and Track & Field. Al's approach to coaching, which he details in the following pages, is as much mental as it is physical, maybe more so. It centers on a deep belief and confidence—what Al calls "the knowing"—where regardless of the conditions or level of competition, you knew on a deep, almost automatic level that you were going to run a great race.

It may sound clichéd—this mind over matter mentality—but Al has spent the last half century doing just that, helping runners understand "the knowing," maximize their God-given talents, and compete selflessly. The results speak for themselves. North Central had decades of teams comprised of runners who, on their own, had few individual accolades. But once Al put them together, something special happened.

It may come as a surprise to some to learn that the North Central cross country and track & field program has never been about "winning," per se. In the Merner Fieldhouse locker room, we had a sign that said, "We Refuse to be Outworked." Not "We Refuse to Lose." Whenever a freshman asked about this, Al would say, "We can't control what other teams do. What happens if Augustana College gets five Kenyans on their team?" We would be the toughest, the most disciplined, the team that trained in every kind of weather, on every kind of surface. Other teams might have more talent and, yes, they might even beat us, but no team would toe the starting line more prepared, physically and mentally, than North Central College.

Winning was a result of Al's program, not a goal.

Al was a legendary figure in my household. My father, Vernon Martin, was a member of North Central's first national championship team in 1975. As a result, I grew up hearing stories about Al and the team. I met Al for the first time when I was still in middle school, not long after I'd completed my inaugural season of cross country. He asked if I liked running. I was still new at it, but I answered that I more than liked it.

"I love it."

He smiled, a grin so broad his eyes nearly closed.

"Then come to North Central!"

Six years later, I did, ready to contribute what I could to one of the country's most storied athletic programs. Admittedly, this wasn't much. I never broke 19 minutes for 5,000 meters in high school, but your level of ability didn't matter at North Central. For decades, the team's unofficial motto has been "Run for Fun and Personal Bests." Talent was irrelevant. If you loved to run and were willing to work hard and work selflessly, North Central's team had a place for you.

My four years at North Central were an interesting time for the program, to put it mildly. Going back to the creation of NCAA Division III in 1973, North Central had finished out of the top four just once at the national championships. Nonetheless, my freshman year we were 12th in the nation. Sophomore year, 13th. Junior year, 16th. It was easy for me, and others, to wonder "What in the world happened?"

It was a period of anxious soul-searching, both inside the program and among its large alumni community. Why had the team repeatedly stumbled after decades of consistent success? Had the "magic" worn off? Had other teams somehow finally figured us out? It could have easily devolved into panicked flailing, and indeed there were many among us who advocated a radical change in the program. New training techniques. A shift in culture from running for fun to running to win. Implementing a time trial or some other way to ensure that not just anyone could join the team.

Instead, Al went "Back to the Basics," as he puts it in this memoir. Reflecting on what he'd learned from his mentors, on his own path to finding joy in running, he reviews his sometimes trial-and-error approach to building the track & field and cross country programs at North Central. The heart of this journey—his building blocks for success in running and life—are laid out in this book. Throughout, he explains candidly how the cultural foundation of North Central's programs began with the lessons he learned from his family, mentors, church, and boyhood experiences and how, as a result of this spiritual melting pot, he has come to equate the word "team" with "love."

And that's what this book is—a love letter. It's for his teams and all the collective miles they've run to better themselves and earn the privilege of wearing North Central's iconic red and white striped jerseys. It's for Ted Haydon, Billy Mills, and the others he credits for inspiring and encouraging him on this journey. It's to God for guiding him to North Central, and a remembrance of all he's learned and absorbed on the way, and everything that makes running special—the wind through your hair, the lightness of your feet, the crisp leaves on the ground and the dew on the grass the morning of a cross country race.

As Al says, "The basic responsibility of a teacher and coach should never veer from the goal of stressing core internal values that guide athletes to personal growth." Competing for North Central made me a better person. The lessons I learned on the track and the cross country course and all the miles in between—I've been able to apply those to nearly every facet of my life, every single day. And every single day I thank Al Carius for it.

Frank Martin
Communications Content Coordinator
J.M. Huber Corporation
North Central Cross Country
and Track & Field,
Class of 2009

Preface

"In a world that's becoming more materialistic, more professional, more outcome-oriented, we believe, to the contrary, that the ultimate competition is you against you."

—Coach Al Carius

"What lies behind us and what lies before us are tiny matters compared to what lies within us."

—Ralph Waldo Emerson

I began to write this book at a confusing time for me and for our cross country program at North Central College (NCC) in Naperville, Illinois. Regularly one of the top national teams in NCAA Division III cross country, my North Central College team had just placed 12th in the 2005 Division III in cross country among the 24 teams competing.

Baffling in a way was my choosing to write this book at that time, when we as a team did not perform at our best. Logically, readers of this book would seem far more interested in reading about our NCC running program following one of our 19 NCAA national titles in cross country or possibly after one of our 12 NCAA National Championships in track & field. Come to think of it, we've had many finishes in second, third, and fourth place nationally, and any *one* of those top four national finishes in cross country would appear to be a better guide to the "secrets" behind our successful running program—the step-by-step process of developing athletes' talent, maximizing individuals' potential, and leading to trophy finishes for our NCC team. Contrary to what the outside world might expect, upon looking back now and knowing what I believe internally, this may have been the perfect time to begin writing this book, when we seemed to have lost our way. Throughout our history, how did North Central College progress from "good to great" at the national level in cross country and track & field, and what factors had helped to prevent our program from encountering the very common slide from "great to good"? Then, what (if anything) went wrong in our program—*what was I doing wrong as a coach*—in the mid-2000s that led to several down years for our NCC runners? And finally, what did I do, what did I change as a college coach and a guide for my athletes that brought our program back to robust health after those disappointing years? Those are legitimate questions which I will try to answer in this book.

But let me be clear from the start. As far as I am concerned, this book is not about trophies and championships. It's ultimately about much more important goals and lasting rewards for the student athletes who built and benefit from our program. From my point of view, the best part of having a successful athletic program is that it gives credibility to our method of helping young people to grow and gain confidence. Our athletic success draws attention to the valuable by-products for our youth derived from their *pursuit* of personal bests in sports and in other areas of their own lives.

This book also lays out a recipe, a path forward, for the many young people today trying to find their way in life. As you'll read below, my friend Jim Braun—a guidance coun-

selor at our local Waubonsie Valley High School—identified
the biggest problem his students face today: "Students today
have lofty goals but most of them do not have a clue as to
the steps necessary to navigate from where they are today
to the achievement of those goals." He seemed to suggest
that many young people seem to have knowledge but lack
a compass, and a map, to help guide them in the pursuit of
their personal goals.

Here is my map, in this book. I train cross country runners and track & field athletes, but this recipe, this process,
should work for any athlete in any sport. I also believe it can
guide other young people pursuing a personal goal in school,
at work, or in their personal lives, who are asking themselves,
"I know where I want to go, but how do I get there?"

Here, broadly, are stories about how young athletes
came to North Central and learned our approach for how
to achieve their personal goals. They acquired the *process*
of how to repeatedly achieve personal bests. Many of them
made themselves champions within their sport. And most
of them went on to be champions in the sport of life. I
think their stories merit sharing, and the lessons are worth
learning. But first, as you will see, their coach had a few life
lessons of his own to learn.

It seems to me that the recipe to success and long-term
growth and development—in sports and in life—is as follows. Know yourself. Know where you want to go. Let nothing external distract you. Surround yourself with supportive
people—*your* team—sharing similar goals. Believe in who
you are, and turn your faith to follow what Dr. Maxwell
Maltz called your internal "servo-mechanism." This is the
path to becoming the best you can be. But to be clear, the
path traveled must be on a rock-solid foundation.

In sports, throughout the process of training and competition, the improvement in an athlete's performance and cardiovascular fitness will become apparent with the physiological changes made by their training. This performance improvement will be accompanied by a feeling of pride and elevated confidence. These personal achievements can lead young people to the discovery of their deeper selves and rooted powers within their soul, and the connection between the body and the mind—the spirit within. Someone who knew and appreciated this spirit and its gift in life once said, "The best things in life can't be seen or touched but are felt in the heart."

As I say in Chapter 3, "I believe that the standards we should teach represent the nonnegotiable, eternal core truths that guide us throughout our lives. Absolute core concepts and ethics become a foundational 'blueprint' for our rules for life as well as a support during adversity along the way. These behavioral ideals leading the athlete to personal bests are inseparable from the ideals for being the best you can be in life."

For me, this moment in 2005 after a less-than-great cross country season was the perfect time to begin to reevaluate my foundational philosophy, our methods, the spiritual nature of running, and the key factors behind the authentic long-term success of our North Central College cross country and track & field programs. Again, I want to be explicit that my purpose as a coach is not about winning, but rather about our student-athletes becoming "Winners in Life" through the physical in the pursuit of success.

Statistics, places, times, labels, and trophies cannot and *should not* objectively measure what is most eternal and enduring in a philosophically led athletic program. Self-discovery, personal growth, and self-realization for the athletes, guided by coached experiences throughout the process, is our goal. My yardstick and definition of success for students and athletes at North Central College is, "Making the most of one's God-given talent." This is Life's benchmark. I like how Albert Einstein put it: "Strive not to be a success but rather to be of value."

This is a concept seemingly being lost within the world of sports in our society. The *best* of athletics is what the experience can do to have a positive, lasting impact on the athlete's life, and not what the athlete can do for the sport and the coach in the pursuit of winning. All of the factors necessary to enrich and to inspire one's athletes to be their best are the ultimate responsibility of the coach, especially one with over 50 years of experience.

Introduction

"The season of failure is the best time for
sowing the seeds of success."

–Paramahansa Yogananda

"Our success is based on 'lots of little differences.'"

–Coach Al Carius

When I took the time to consider our disappointing 2005 cross country season, our mistakes—my mistakes—became clear. The overall effort of that year's North Central team was not lacking. They had done the physical work and what was asked of them. But, my review of our team-building process and internal preparation revealed numerous factors that weakened our competitive culture and prevented us from being at our best in the end. The story of what we did wrong in the years leading up to 2005, what we did right with our teams for many years before, and what we have tried to do correctly in the years since, make up the frame of this book. Within that frame, I discuss the history of our NCC program, and some of my own, and the guiding principles like Purpose, the Spirit, and Culture that help to make individuals and teams great.

Historically, our first NCAA National Championship arrived in the fall of 1975 with a team we called the "No Names." In 1973 and 1974, we had placed second and third in the nation

1

in Division III cross country with teams led by two of our best All-American runners, Glenn Behnke and Scott Barrett. The No Names who brought us our first championship were different. Individually, each runner had few impressive running credentials, but amazingly, together they were synergistically elevated to great team performances with every race. Many of these same athletes, with the addition of some more No Names, won a second national championship the following year. A question I long pondered was, "What invisible advantage did this group of average athletes have that made them so successful as a team?" Our physical workouts had been similar for many years. But I knew there was something more. What was their—our—secret?

I have been asked this question so many times, I finally came up with a glib, but accurate, answer: "Lots of little differences." I borrowed this phrase from the side of a Hy-Vee Grocery store delivery truck I saw in Grinell, Iowa in 1993. We had just won the national championship cross country meet there in Grinell, and Hy-Vee's motto at the time seemed a good short-hand answer to the question, "Why has your team just won *another* championship?" Our success is based upon "Lots of little differences," I learned to say. And indeed it is. I keep a miniature Hy-Vee truck on my desk to remind me that no single workout or tactic or person is the key to our success, but "Lots of little differences." What differences? I hope you'll see them as your read further.

Here is one problem I discovered after our teams later had some disappointing years. Since that first national championship in 1975, I had mistakenly thought we had the secret physical training formula and were on auto pilot, built around our string of national trophy finishes that followed. Simply put, our consistency of top four finishes, including 24 first and second place finishes in 32 years, had lulled me into a false conclusion that our workouts were magic. I developed a misguided assumption that all our athletes *arrived* at college intrinsically motivated—assuring outstanding team performances just by plugging in a new class of freshmen athletes yearly into our "perfect" physical training system. Plainly, way back then I had no idea of the unseen complexity and inner depth involved in successful team performance.

It should be noted at this point that my faulty, superficial thinking about the ease of our success was based on my one-dimensional belief in our mechanistic, science-based workouts—the physical aspects of our program. To be sure, overall our training was based upon physiologically sound training concepts. But, unknown to me at the time, the real foundation for our consistency of success at North Central was linked to our fundamental philosophical core value system—our culture, the right culture, based upon the source for absolute truth.

It is clear to me now that today's hectic world of ongoing changes has created greater distractions and stressors for our athletes than during the era I experienced on my teams in the 1960s and '70s. As far as I am concerned, today's youth are facing a technological bombardment of ideas, exposing their minds too often to unfavorable mental "junk food" through the internet, movies, television, music, magazines, and video games, to name but a few. For those student-athletes without firm, internal, core anchors, this dark side of our culture and its mixed messages can cause negative social consequences, great confusion, and poor personal choices that adversely affect their lives. Unfortunately, many students seem unaware of teachings from the likes of the great Ralph Waldo Emer-

3

son: "Nothing can bring you peace but yourself. Nothing can bring you peace but the triumph of principles."

Certainly, the competition for the hearts and minds of young people from their surrounding environment has drastically changed from the conservative world in which I grew up in Morton, Illinois, and from what my earliest teams experienced. Had this mental "junk food" and the resulting confusion in our athletes' minds crept in and affected our teams' performances? Stability and harmony are created when one's subconscious mindset is consistent with one's conscious values and behaviors. This is true for all of us as individuals and for great teams as well. "There is no pillow as soft as a clear conscience," is how Coach John Wooden put it.

I recognized over time that the fruitful cultural foundation of our North Central Cross Country and Track & Field program has always been rooted in the deep, inner, and timeless core standards I experienced and absorbed through my family, church, and education while a young boy growing up in Morton, Illinois. I have always believed the saying, "You are a part of every experience you have had and every person you have met throughout your life."

Much of who I am and the rules of behavior that guide me I absorbed as a young boy. Most of what I know about coaching I learned in Sunday School. These well-defined and clear boundaries were modeled for me consistently at home, at church, and in school, teaching me eternal truths of right and wrong, good, and bad, as well as basic manners like saying, "Please" and "Thank you." I learned timeless truths and simple guidelines for my behavior, but they proved immensely valuable steps toward finding my ideal best self.

It seems to me that too many of these once pure boundaries within our society have been diluted by the spread of a more worldly perspective. Family, church, and education have been undermined and compromised, obscuring a unified message to young people. This message concerns the appropriate values that should be taught to young people to lead them to becoming their best selves.

Unmistakably, at the center of teaching me those moral principles was my family's church, the conservative Apostolic Christian Church—an offshoot of the Amish church. In our church, God's spiritual "blueprint" was taught through Biblical teachings and lived by our adhering to timeless ethical values. To be sure, these moral absolute truths I was taught led me to my stated definition of success for our athletes—making the most of your God-given gifts and talents.

My own version of this definition became our team motto, "Run for Fun and Personal Bests." By defining our goal in this way, success is universally available to any athlete in our program through the freedom of their own choices. When you think about this definition of success and our motto, you can see that a specific outcome—a qualifying time or a top finish—is never guaranteed. But *success* is accessible to every individual, founded on their voluntary choices each day to better themselves through self-growth. Athletes seek *personal* best performances each week, each season, and can enjoy success by reaching their personal goals, by competing solely against themselves, with the support of their teammates. It doesn't matter if they are the fastest or the slowest member of our team. Our team benefits and our culture benefits—we get better and better as a team—as our individual athletes focus their energy to seek their personal goals through patient daily improvement.

5

Some years back, there was a time when I concluded that these core team virtues—work hard enough to do your best, help your teammates to be their best—were accepted as ongoing intrinsic standards and beliefs by all of our runners. I took for granted that they were passed down responsibly from one class to the next internally, almost automatically, through our upper-class leaders to the newcomers each year. I was mistaken.

Over time, it seems to me that man's social and situational ethics have slowly weakened our society in America and eroded some of our collectively accepted codes of conduct. In my opinion, I allowed these same social changes to undermine our culture on our North Central College teams. Let's face it, it's a changing world, and some things do not stay the same. Not surprisingly, our consistently strong performances in cross country at the national level through 2004 had lulled me into complacency. I could not see, or I was in denial about, some of these internal trends transforming our teams and the gradual entropic erosion of our foundational cardinal virtues. Our program was on the brink, and I did not recognize it at the time.

Finally, intuitively, I sensed a slow gravitation away from the fundamental, time-proven spiritual base of our success. This process of self-evaluation and self-discovery began after our 2005 team's 12th place finish at the Division III National Championships. That difficult year made evident to me the importance of refocusing myself and our team on those firm, internal, spiritual and moral standards we had fostered for so many years, but that I had allowed to drift away. As I later discovered, this insight was correct, but much time was necessary to effectively rebuild what had actually been the bedrock of the success of our program. There was to be no quick fix. Turns out that, to a great extent, we had continued to focus solely on the physical aspects of performance while ignoring the essential component of our previous success— the right culture for our team. The culture, or driving spirit, of the team is the internal connecting glue—and collective bond—to unite the athlete's body, mind, and heart. We were failing and had to find the path back to knowing who we are, as individuals and a team. "Knowing yourself," said Aristotle, "is the beginning of wisdom."

After the 2005 season, I responded to my soul searching with our theme for 2006, "Back to the Basics." I personally took full responsibility for the decline of our culture and the standards I knew innately are so necessary for enabling our athletes to succeed, to connect with their inner intuitive wisdom to achieve their personal bests. After all, our athletes had at most only four years of involvement at the collegiate level while, at the time, I had over 40 years of experience within the same program. Clearly, most of our runners have always given their very best. From my perspective, analyzing our substandard performance in 2005 was vital to my acknowledgment of, and accepting responsibility for, the cracks that had crept into our program's foundation. Dr. Dennis Waitley described the choices I had: "There are two primary choices in life: To accept conditions as they exist, or accept the responsibility for changing them."

Remarkably, one of the valuable benefits of 50 years of coaching at North Central College has been the feedback from trial and error, and even from our failures. To begin to understand and correct a problem, one must be flexible, adaptable, creative, and humble to recognize the unique problems faced by our student athletes in these rapidly changing times and to transform weakness into strength. Yet, in the process, the basic responsibility of a teacher and coach should never veer from the objective of stressing core, enduring, foundational values that guide athletes toward self-development. The final authority for communicating these values remains with the head coach. To be effective, the message cannot be outsourced.

Intriguing to me was the outcome of the next year's national championship at Wilmington College in Ohio. While we were working that year to regain our cultural footing, the 2006 Calvin College cross country team openly demonstrated this internal cohesiveness—the joining of one's body, mind, and spirit—I was trying to re-instill in our own teams. Calvin's team produced a near-record-setting performance under the worst running conditions I have ever seen during my 50 years of coaching at NCC. Pure mud and, in some spots, knee-deep water covered the entire 8,000-meter course.

Five minutes before the start, two of our athletes warmed up past me and commented independently on the lack of traction and overall terrible conditions on this normally fast course. By this time, nearly all of the teams were having similar physical and mental reactions to the mud, anticipating havoc for times and performances. Clearly our North Central College athletes did not have positive expectations for our race process or our final results that day. As William James noted, "It is our attitude at the beginning of a difficult task which, more than anything else, will affect its successful outcome."

In my opinion, that feeling was shared by every team on that muddy course that day—except one. At that national meet, one team unmistakably dominated the competition with mind, body, heart, and spirit blended for deep, inner, positive expectations and confidence we call "the knowing." Calvin College, the meet favorite, stayed focused and won confidently with just 37 points, only five away from the meet record of 32 set by North Central's 1993 team. I believe our North Central team was beaten, mentally, before the gun went off at the start. On that day, I did not refocus their thoughts nor reduce their doubts with my leadership.

From all I could tell, Calvin's team performance was synergistically fortified. Their athletes adhered to their team's core principles and beliefs, embracing these important factors that lead to team success. All of our great teams, regardless of their final outcome, reach this automatic internal state of focused unity and are oblivious to distractions like mud and rain, allowing them to perform in the moment to the best of their "God-given talent."

In contrast, North Central College's young team in 2006 was maturing and growing, through slowly reconnecting to our foundational core ideals. Our team's attitude was returning to the theme "Back to the Basics," but that was not reflected objectively on the 2006 Wilmington course where we slipped to a 13th place finish. Yet, on this day, our place was not my biggest concern. It was insignificant in comparison to our on-going, improving, internal growth that year, which would soon give us our opportunity to be back at our best again. That season was at best a reinforcement of the new beginning for our program of the day-by-day process of re-emphasizing primary, foundational, core ideals within our team. I knew our culture was once again heading in the right direction, but it would take time and time cannot be rushed. I had to continue patiently restructuring our culture through what I was communicating and, more importantly, by what I did.

While at the awards ceremony for our All-American Nick Hird, I was congratulating the two outstanding Calvin College national championship coaches, Brian Diemer and Al Hoekstra, on their great team's performance. True to the class that surrounds their program, Coach Al Hoekstra removed any lingering doubt in my mind about our team's direction by responding, "We modeled our program after North Central College."

What follows are my memories and thoughts about the values, influences, and variables which represent our definition of success, "Making the most of your God-given talents," and our motto, "Run for Fun and Personal Bests."

CHAPTER 1

Run for Fun and Personal Bests

"All the talent and knowledge in the world won't
help a young person if he or she doesn't learn
how to adopt and apply it."

—Coach Al Carius

"Make the most of yourself, for that
is all there is of you."

—Ralph Waldo Emerson

Four of my five children—Rick, Stephanie, Brent, and Sam—attended Waubonsie Valley High School near North Central College. My oldest son Scott graduated from Naperville North High School. On one occasion, I had the opportunity to speak to a guidance counselor at Waubonsie named Jim Braun. Making conversation, I asked Jim, "What is the number one problem you deal with as a guidance counselor?" It turns out, I was very surprised by his answer. I had expected him to say, "lack of discipline, alcohol, drugs," or something along those lines. Instead, he said, "Students today have lofty goals but most of them do not have a clue as to the steps necessary to navigate from where they are today to the achievement of those goals."

I pondered that surprising statement for a long time, and tried to relate it to coaching at the collegiate level. Runners and track and field athletes may have all the physical tools they need to be a success. But without an understanding of the moment-by-moment process they need to follow in order to succeed—the necessary work, attitude, motivation, and foundation they need to build—they may never attain their goals. All the talent and knowledge in the world won't help a young person if he or she doesn't learn how to adopt and apply it.

"The greatest discovery of my generation," wrote the American philosopher William James, "is that a human being can alter his life by altering his attitudes." I embrace James's statement, and I also believe John Wooden, the legendary UCLA basketball coach, was right years ago when he suggested that you build an athlete from the inside out. What I am suggesting is, there is an order for life providing the best path to navigate to your goals—maximizing your potential with successive personal bests.

"Run for Fun and Personal Bests" is the simple yet powerful message giving vision to, and establishing the framework for, the foundation of our track & field and cross country culture at North Central College. For our athletes, this motto is my answer to the question Waubonsie Valley counselor Jim Braun raised. How does an athlete navigate step-by-step, persistently, from where they are today to the achievement of their "lofty goals"? Compete for fun. Enjoy the journey. Establish a personal intrinsic goal or target. Don't compare yourself or your performance to others. Focus your commitment on the development of internal personal strengths. Strive for *personal* bests. And as Emerson said, "Make the most of yourself, for that is all there is of you."

Our motto's true meaning has been and continues to be my standard, a simple guiding light, giving me clarity when making specific decisions for our athletes and our program. This code of ethics is consistent with the ideals of the NCAA Division III, of North Central College education, and of my own life. Athletics ideally are an integral part of the whole educational experience. Simply put, athletics at its best is not extracurricular but rather part of a curricular "living education," providing a laboratory of experiments *through trial and error experience* to help student-athletes reach for their goals as an athlete and in life. "All life is an experiment," Emerson reminded us. "The more experiments you have, the better."

Through the years, why were some of our runners failing to fully understand the fundamental, foundational significance beneath our motto? Really, the failure was with my lack of consistent, clear communication regarding the meaning of the message within those words. I needed to ensure that the separate statements "Run for Fun" and "Run for Personal Bests" would be understood in the way I intended it. And I needed to remember, as President Ronald Reagan said about our freedom, that our *culture* is never more than one generation away from extinction.

There is not much doubt that to coach effectively you must be explicit in your intent daily, and follow through faithfully each year to redefine and explain your values meaningfully. Phillippa Lally, a health psychology researcher at University College, London, has stated, "It will probably take from two months to eight months to build a new behavior into your life." So it was necessary for me to be explicit, repetitive, and persistent in stressing the values I thought important for my teams. In the past, I had left this important process to chance, assuming our message was being passed down internally within the team. The responsibility was mine. The solution had to be mine too. At this point, it might be helpful to explain how my own experience as an athlete led me to develop this important information at the heart of our successful North Central College program.

The philosophy of this foundation of our track & field and cross country program at NCC has been a constant since I arrived at North Central College in the fall of 1966. "Run for Fun and Personal Bests." I formulated this motto as both a contrast and a reflection of all my teachers and coaches throughout my life, blending them together and thus creating my own philosophy. Interestingly, two highly successful coaches on opposite ends of the philosophical spectrum had the greatest influence on me—my coach, Bill Easton, at the University of Kansas during my first semester as a freshman in the fall of 1960 and later, Coach Ted Haydon of the University of Chicago Track Club.

It's clear to me now that, when I was a young man in school, all high school sports were connected to the whole educational mission. This is what I grew up with, so this is what I considered normal when I chose a college and became a coach myself. I loved sports. I went from season to season, playing four years of basketball, four years of track, two years of baseball (at the same time as track), two years of football, and two years of cross country. I think it's unfortunate that many parents and coaches today think that young people should specialize in just one sport from a very young age in order to "succeed" in sports. With this varied sports background, I had lots of fun in many sports, developed all-around fitness, learned many lessons about teamwork and hard work, and still ended up being a decent runner in the end. As I discovered, through trials and a lot of error, I was better matched for running, and my love for running helped me produce several personal best performances. I placed sixth and second in the Illinois State Cross Country Championship meet my junior and senior years. My senior year in track, I won the State mile, after running a 4:18.4 mile earlier in the spring. This time attracted the attention of the University of Kansas coach, Bill Easton, who ultimately offered me an athletic scholarship.

When I thought I was ready to leave Morton, Illinois, attend college, and take my running career to the next level, I decided, superficially at the time, that Coach Easton's Kansas program would be the best choice for me. Soon enough, I was leaving my home base of Morton and on my way to Lawrence, Kansas. I mistakenly thought I was mature and ready to be away from home, but soon found out that I needed more time and maturity for the transition from high school to college. From my very first day, I knew that I had made a hasty choice, and I was not feeling comfortable with my decision. I learned the hard way what Emerson knew: "The years teach much which the days never know."

The leadership approach of Coach Easton seemed to me to be focused on what the athlete could do for the primary goal of outcome and winning. I determined quickly that, for me, there was substance missing in this approach. I learned first-hand how hard it is to be happy and successful at something when you are not intrinsically motivated, when you personally do not create your own goal internally. Granted, I was very immature, naïve, and homesick at the time. That being so, I did not adapt well to this business approach to running.

In my mind, being homesick was no less of an illness than having a cold or the flu. It affected me the same way any disease would: basically, draining my energy and making me feel lonely. I missed Morton and was constantly trying to find out what was happening with high school sports in central Illinois, how the family Dairy Queen was faring, and what was going on in the lives of my high school friends and family. This was long before the days of cell phones or the internet, so I felt even more isolated in my own new world away from my home base.

What was once my release soon soured as well. At Kansas, I was running well, with our Freshman team winning the Big Eight and National Postal Cross Country Championships, while I won the Big Eight individual title. But running no longer was fun for me and my attitude suffered immensely. Accepting a scholarship as a motive to attend college was a huge mistake for me, and I recognized it more with every passing day. Running had become a job and not a joy for me. I was losing my passion, and I wanted to run for pure intrinsic satisfaction and the joy of the sport again. But I was afraid that without the scholarship, I couldn't afford college. I was also apprehensive of quitting and heading back to Morton to be perceived as a failure.

Yet, even though running at Kansas produced a negative experience for me, ultimately it had great benefits in helping me know myself better and form my philosophy. Instead of focusing on the joys of running, we were consistently reminded of our Kansas scholarship and the responsibilities that went along with it. Running for the Kansas program,

I had lost my feeling for the reasons I had competed in high school. I had lost something deep inside of me and the intrinsic love of running, the love of running free. It eventually occurred to me that something had to change. I had to take a deeper look within to make that change. With self-examination and self-reflection, I made the decision to transfer to another university. I will never forget the day I visited Coach Easton and told him of my decision. We met for two hours from 3 to 5 p.m. on a Friday afternoon. He very bluntly told me that I was making the biggest mistake of my life and that if I went through with it, I would regret it and someday write him a letter telling him I made a mistake and that he had been right. I left his office with very mixed emotions, and feeling confused and frustrated. It was not Coach Easton's fault. It was purely mine for really not examining *who I was* before choosing a college.

I knew I was making the right decision to leave, but I was disconnected and doubtful about the future. All I am saying is that my coach had brought out depths of shortcomings in me that I didn't even think were possible for an 18-year-old to encounter.

As I sat in my dorm room packing and preparing for how I was going to explain my sudden return to Morton, after one semester, to my family, my high school coach, and my friends, I was visited serendipitously by an angel on earth by the name of Billy Mills. Billy was a teammate of mine, a tribal member of the Lakota Nation [Sioux] who had also come to the University of Kansas on an athletic scholarship from the Pine Ridge Indian Reservation in South Dakota. Billy was simply one of the most promising distance runners in the United States at the time, and went on to become the Olympic Champion at 10,000 Meters in Tokyo in 1964. He was orphaned as a young boy growing up on the Pine Ridge Indian Reservation, and the primary way he received a college education was through an athletic scholarship. Billy listened to my explanation of why I was leaving. Then, in a great act of kindness, Billy explained to me that, if he could afford to leave the university, he would too. His college running had become a business to him as well, but it was his path to an education.

This angel on earth, the great Billy Mills, applauded my decision and assured me that it was the right and only choice for me to make. That brief discussion with a wise teammate reinforced my gut feeling. I knew if I were ever to find joy in running again, I had to leave Kansas. To this day, I have never regretted my decision, and I never wrote the letter to Coach Easton. [Note: The movie *Running Brave* is the story of Billy Mills's life and running career.]

I went home, and chose the University of Illinois (U of I) to continue my college education and running career. I was excited about my decision to attend my home-state university, but very concerned about the possibility of again failing to choose a school for my education and a running program where I would enjoy running again. Due to NCAA rules, I was ineligible to compete for the U of I for all of 1961, including the fall 1961 cross country season. During that year, I trained with the Illini distance runners, competed unattached in some open meets sponsored by the University of Chicago Track Club (UCTC), and grew to understand myself better. Most importantly, it was during that year of ineligibility that my love of running returned. How? What changed for me, and how did what I found affect me when I became a coach?

18

Have you ever been touched by an innocent event that rekindled a spark deep within you from a past you thought you had lost? An example that always grabs me is the closing scene in the movie "Field of Dreams" when Kevin Costner says, "Dad, do you want to have a catch?" That, of course, always reminds me of how much I miss my father, especially having him around to watch me—or my teams—compete.

In my first year at U of I, I had one of those innocent moments while running across campus with my new teammates one quiet October evening. The beauty of the fall was everywhere as Lance Herning, Stan Ripskis, Harold Harris, Jim McElwee, and I ran down one of the winding paths of the cemetery just east of Memorial Stadium. The air was crisp. The haze of burning leaves filtered the setting sun and the colors of autumn reflected off every tree and under each stride, creating a hypnotic effect as we talked and ran.

For some reason, we were discussing athletic scholarships. My experience at Kansas and my naïveté had led me to believe that every athlete in college was on some sort of athletic scholarship and was competing at least in part because of this extrinsic financial motivation. I remember the exact spot, as we headed toward the street and the locker room in Huff Gymnasium, where my friends informed me that they were *not* on any athletic scholarships! A light went on in my heart.

I was completely taken aback and inquired of them, "Do you mean to tell me that you are not receiving money and are out here running because you love to run?" Their answer was a resounding "Yes," and for the first time I finally got it. Here, running next to me, were four teammates who were running in college not because they *had* to but because they *wanted* to, because they loved to.

19

Truth is, I was shocked, and inspired, to find myself again with athletes who were running because of what they felt on the *inside* rather than what they were getting on the outside! In that moment, I rediscovered the intrinsic freedom of play and fun of Morton athletics that I had lost along the way. "For the love of the game. For the love of the sport." In an era when too often the external has become the focus, where "more" or "money" seems to be the answer, I on that lovely autumn evening reconnected with the innocence and childhood beauty of *running as play*. I witnessed, I re-experienced, pure love and joy in running for running's sake. The ultimate reward is not the prize, but the internal satisfaction of improvement and the joy of sharing the experience with others in the brotherhood of running and fun! Running for all the wrong reasons takes so much away from our beautiful sport.

I have to note too that falling back in love with running was clearly beneficial for my personal performances. Running happily at the U of I, I became a three-time Big Ten two-mile Champion and two-time Big Ten cross country Champion.

"Without exception, Ted Haydon always put people before victory and athletes before the sport. I wanna be more like Ted Haydon!"

—*Coach Al Carius*

So, 1961 ended up being a great year for me, after returning to run for Illinois, for it was also the year when I met my mentor, Ted Haydon, who modeled and guided me on the path to my North Central College running philosophy. I had been introduced to Coach Ted Haydon through

20

my Illinois coaches Leo Johnson and Olympic Steeplechaser Phil Coleman. I got to know Ted well at the University of Chicago, where I raced in open track meets while ineligible.

As the head coach at the University of Chicago and the organizer, administrator, and coach of the University of Chicago Track Club (UCTC), Ted Haydon had a tremendous impact on me as a coach, and as a person. During my 50 years of coaching, when I might have had doubts about the path to take, I have regularly reminded myself, as I look beside me at his picture on my wall: "What would Ted say or do in this situation?"

I began competing regularly with the UCTC after graduating from Illinois and entering their graduate school, serving as a graduate assistant for Coach Leo Johnson (1964-65) and Coach Bob Wright (1965-66) while in the undergraduate physical education program. Running for UCTC, I developed tremendous respect for Coach Haydon—both for his knowledge of the sport, and far more importantly, for his coaching philosophy. His approach was completely opposite from what I had experienced in my first semester at Kansas under Coach Easton.

Ted Haydon put the athlete's well-being and growth first in every decision he made within his track and cross country programs. His focus and decisions were always made with the thought, "How can this experience in track and cross country have a positive influence on the participants' lives? How can it help athletes change and grow through the experience?" In other words, "What can the sport and the coach do for the athlete?" rather than, "What can the athlete do for the sport or the coach?" Coach Haydon always realized that participation in sports was a means to an end and not an end in itself.

So, there was little wonder that Coach Haydon opened his athletic door to post-collegiate athletes who desired to continue running and competing. All these athletes had two things in common: the love of the sport and a desire to continue to participate under Ted Haydon's leadership. Intrinsically, they chose to be a part of a track and cross country program with someone who valued their passion and appreciated their diversity and uniqueness as individuals. Consequently, it is easy to understand that the University of Chicago Track Club banquet each year was a wonderful, unique event—a blend of men and women, young and old, collegiate and post-collegiate, and Olympians as well as completely unknown athletes with little natural talent. All were brought together by the bond of the amateur code—love of sport.

Ted Haydon provided athletes with the opportunity to compete in one of the most selfless ways I have ever witnessed in the field of athletics. Let's just say qualification for Ted's track club (UCTC) was never based on times or performance but rather always on *attitude*. As a young athlete and future coach, this had a tremendous impact on me and I've embraced this philosophical approach within our own program ever since. Consider for a moment one of the many lessons and statements I remember Ted saying about his eclectic University of Chicago track club while at a Division one dual meet: "You know Al, we really do not want to win any of these meets we compete in. Because if we win, we will never be invited back."

Since Haydon wanted to provide opportunities for athletes to compete in competitive meets, he needed his club to be invited back. At that time, UCTC had dual meets with the likes of the University of Michigan, the University of

Wisconsin, and the University of Iowa—outstanding competition for the club's unattached and Olympic-level athletes. For other athletes of all ages and varying talent, Ted would also provide endless numbers of open meet opportunities at U of C, just to give athletes an avenue to compete for the pure love of track and cross country. Having recently come out of two Division I running programs, and being a young adult entering into a world where the goals too often only seemed to be "to win" or to enhance the coach's reputation, I was greatly inspired by Ted's selfless ideas.

Without exception, Ted Haydon always put people before victory and athletes before the sport. From Ted, I learned that coaching is not solely about how to make better runners. It's also about the experience of helping athletes to learn and grow to be people of character. No question about it, I marveled at Haydon's ability to always say the right thing at the right time. He also knew how to keep a sense of perspective about sports and on other people's interpretations of situations and events. Ted never got wrapped up in rules, but rather focused on any common sense flexibility with adjustments that would benefit the athletes's exposure for internal growth.

I remember Ted in the 1970s deftly handling an "athlete-first" problem while overseeing the Division III national track and field meet in Chicago. There had been rain on the Chicago lakefront, and conditions even on the artificial track were wet. The great (soon to be) 2-time Olympic 400 meter hurdles champion, Edwin Moses, was competing for Division III Morehouse College. Moses, who ultimately would set the world record in the event 4 times, was expected to cruise to victory in the event before representing the US in his first Olympics later in the summer.

Unfortunately, like a number of runners that day, Moses slipped and fell on the wet track during the 400 meter hurdle finals and did not finish! What to do!? The world's greatest 400 meter hurdler was out of the Division III meet. Ted Haydon, always focusing on what was best for the athlete, calmly allowed Moses to re-run the race—a tentative, "consolation race" he called it—with a few other athletes. I remember Ted saying, "He was going to win the race anyway!" Moses as expected ran the fastest time of the day, going away. Coach Haydon then discussed with the meet Rules Committee the possibility of getting Edwin Moses reinstated as the winner of the NCAA Division III hurdle event. Haydon was not about to let the rulebook interfere with what was best for the athlete, and frankly, for the sport.

However, on that day Coach Haydon couldn't convince the NCAA Rules Committee of the justice of his argument, so the world-class time run by Edwin Moses in the consolation race was not allowed to stand. Rules are rules, I guess. Moses went on during the following summer to win the Olympic 400 meter hurdles final in Montreal in a world record time of 47.64. Oddly, Edwin Moses won his Olympic title without ever being an NCAA champion in the event.

Like a modern philosopher, Ted always had the proper point of view of what was really most central in athletic experience. Another great example of this was at the Mexico City Olympics in 1968, where Coach Haydon was the American Olympic distance coach. Jim Ryun, America's top 1,500-meter runner, was walking with Ted to the Olympic Stadium prior to the 1,500-meter final. Ryun asked Ted to "say a little prayer for me." Ted thought for a moment and commented, "Jim, I've decided I'm not going to say a prayer for you." Ryun, mildly surprised, asked why not? "Because," said

Haydon, "I'm going to save that for something important."
Haydon always kept sports in perspective. You pray for the
sick and those less fortunate in their lives, but not for victory
over another in a sport. Another less modern philosopher,
Socrates, said it this way: "Our prayers should be for blessings
in general, for God knows best what is good for us."

Haydon, you see, was interested in helping all of his athletes grow—physically, intellectually, emotionally, socially,
and I believe, in his own way, spiritually—through the
experience of training and competing in sport, regardless
of the outcome. This was his goal with Olympic athletes and
all the others he coached throughout his legendary career,
providing opportunities through competition for them to
mature as people. Haydon knew that running was a means
to an end—the process of self-discovery leading to learning,
growing, and eventually self-mastery. You could never lose
with Ted Haydon, only learn and grow. I, and all my athletes
at North Central, owe him a great debt.

---

*"Our chief want is someone who will inspire us to be
what we know we could be."*
—Ralph Waldo Emerson

Ted Haydon inspired me, and in the spirit of Ted Haydon's wonderful perspective on athletics, I credit our program's motto to the philosophical perspective I learned
from Ted. "Run for Fun and Personal Bests." It sounds
simple, catchy, and perhaps even superficial, but there is a
great depth of exceptional meaning within the motto. First
of all, "Run for Fun" means to do exactly what Ted Haydon
implied to Jim Ryun. Keep perspective on what we are doing.

Running is not war, it is not life or death, it does not determine whether or not the sun will rise the next day, and it
does not determine your worth as a person. Track & field
and cross country are great sports. But, they're just that: a
sport, something that as kids we played for fun.

Here's something I realized when I was racing for the
U of I. This incident helped me to realize the importance
for athletes of learning to pursue personal bests instead of
judging themselves on whether on not they were "winners."
I ran a personal best one spring by breaking the 9-minute
barrier in the two mile run at the Drake Relays. I didn't win
the race, but I did run my fastest time to that point, and was
also the first Big 10 runner to run under 9 minutes. I felt
really good about my performance, but it has always stuck
in my mind that all anyone wanted to know back at school
was why I hadn't won the event!

I mean, here I had achieved a personal best and established a Big 10 conference precedent in the process. But,
because I didn't win, people thought something was wrong.
I myself thought something was wrong with *their* inability
to understand that I had just run a great race! I was very
proud of myself, and that pride in my performance gave
me the incentive to keep working hard to perform even
better next time. I congratulated myself on my performance,
even if others didn't. And this memory helped to convince
me, when I became a coach, to celebrate when my athletes
achieved their own personal bests, no matter where they
placed in any race. The real goal for athletes (and people
in other walks of life, frankly) should be to continually
improve yourself, regardless of winning. And the key to that
is keeping it fun, and keeping your running and jumping
and throwing in perspective.

Consider this story. A few years ago, before the NCAA Division III Indoor National Championships, an athlete from the University of Wisconsin–Stevens Point was expected to win the 800-meter race. A reporter asked the athlete, David Litsheim, if he was nervous about being the favorite to win the 800-meter title. Litsheim was a veteran who had served our country during a tour of duty in Afghanistan, and his answer is another good example of keeping the importance of sports in perspective. "No, this is a track meet, and I have nothing to be nervous about. This is fun! Now when I was in Afghanistan and the enemy was shooting bullets at me, then I was nervous."

The perspective of "Run for Fun and Personal Bests" can be traced directly back to my association with Ted Haydon. He taught me that running is a means to a greater end than times, places, points, accolades, or trophies; that the simple act of running really is not an end in itself. Beyond all question, there are certainly many things much bigger and more important in life than running, so running at its best is to be a part of one's life, a pathway to a more significant life, but not one's whole life.

To that end, running should be a means through which athletes learn core life lessons while having fun. The fun and joy will intrinsically come from the satisfaction of playing the sport while accumulating many unique qualities that lead to self-growth in the company of teammates and friends. Increasingly in colleges and, worse, in youth sports programs across America, we seem to be taking the "play" out of playing sports. Even the super-successful Chicago Bear linebacker, Mike Singletary, kept his amazing focus on this important goal, saying, "Do you know what my favorite part of the game is? The opportunity to play."

Like Haydon, my focus is to put the person before the sport, so that while developing runners, I am more notably helping to shape young men for their lives beyond the sport. Decisions for our team that are made daily are based upon putting our athletes in the right culture, training, and meet selections. Here they can experience their best opportunity for improvement and follow the path to reach their potential. Along the way, there will be challenges, adversity, and disappointments. It is all a part of the sport journey and all a part of life. It is during those times that an athlete needs a coach, with his encouragement, the most.

Don Church, a former coach and great friend of mine from Wheaton College in Illinois, coined a phrase for me: "Freedom to fail." He stated that every runner goes into competition to do his or her best, to give it their all. But that runner who gives his best is the same person after the race whether the champion or in last place. Any disappointments and perceived failures along the way are ultimately opportunities to strengthen and fortify character. Character, he argued, is not defined by a time or a place in a race, but rather by how you interpret and respond to your performance. I agree. Emerson said it this way: "Our greatest glory is not in never failing, but in rising up every time we fail."

The second part of our philosophy concerns the essence of life, seeking personal bests. It is imperative to establish a solid atmosphere of trust through honesty, transparency, and reliable communication within the team culture. From this, traditions will evolve that will be and should be passed on from the team's internal upper-class leadership to the newer freshman class. One of these traditions is to recognize and honor any runner for achieving lifetime bests, his personal best performances.

While a student at the University of Illinois, I had the good fortune to have a professor, Dr. Glenn Blair, who was an educational psychologist before there were sport psychologists. Glenn Blair was a master of connecting the mind and the body for a desired result. One of the countless principles he communicated clearly and simply was to always reference and reinforce the desired behavior you were seeking from someone. "For effective learning," Dr. Blair noted, "responses must be immediately reinforced."

Throughout my coaching career, this uncomplicated principle has guided me often when confronting various behaviors from team members. To reinforce our desired behavior, we honor athletes with an NCC Cardinal-head sticker labeled with the greatest honor and recognition we have within our program—"Personal Best." John Wooden once said, "Success is peace of mind knowing that you did your best to become the best that you are capable of becoming."

That sums up simply the goal I have had for North Central College Track and Cross Country for the past 50 years. Track & field and cross country are unique sports in which you can always accurately measure your progress by improved performances. Again, yes, this is a measurable objective outcome for the athlete, but what is most important is the person you become and the reinforcement of the unfathomable life lessons you absorb in seeking your personal bests.

Dan Siewert was a great thrower we had within our track and field program. Years ago, he was competing in one of our "Last Chance" meets prior to the NCAA Championships. We host several of these meets at North Central each year to give athletes from many colleges a final chance to meet NCAA qualifying times, throws, or jumps. This is my way of carrying on another great Ted Haydon tradition: Give athletes from any school or post-collegiate competitors more chances to compete and meet their personal goals. These are fun track meets full of individual athletic performances, since we don't keep team scores, and are open to single athletes from all over the country.

To put this story in context, there were over 1,000 participants in this meet, so it was similar to a three-ring circus with competitions and events scattered throughout our meet site. From this setting, I remember I was having great difficulty keeping up with each of our athlete's performances throughout the day. At one point, one of our coaches saw me and asked, "Did you know Dan won the hammer?" Later, one of Dan's teammates found me and said, "Did you know Dan won the shot-put and set a meet record?" Finally, a fan found me and excitedly shared that Dan had won the discus and qualified for the NCAA National Championships. My response again was that I didn't know of all of Dan's accomplishments—winning three events, setting a record, and qualifying for the national championships.

I couldn't wait to see Dan and congratulate him! Later in that long evening, I came across Dan near the track and said, "Congratulations on your wins and your new record!" He responded, "Thanks Coach! Today I got three personal bests!"

What an affirmation, what a compliment that response was to me! Dan remembered, and reminded me, that his wins and his new meet shot-put record were not his goals and not the goals we set for him. He did not compare himself to anything or anyone external to himself. Dan was proud that he had beaten his toughest competition, his own best performances, three times in one night.

Personal bests do not depend on what your competitors do. Rather, they depend upon one's own dedication to basic concepts such as intrinsic motivation, commitment, focus, work ethic, discipline, and confidence. Running, jumping, or throwing your best—doing your best—depends, in short, on *you*.

As well, I am reminded of the evening I met Herb Elliot, the 1960 Olympic 1,500-meter Champion from Australia. He addressed all of the coaches during an NCAA National Championship held at North Central College in 2000. It was a dream come true for me since Elliot was my idol when I began my distance running back in high school. I was mesmerized by his perspective and his wisdom of life and running. He spoke engagingly about his training under his inspirational coach, Percy Cerutty. Cerutty was a philosophical coach well ahead of his time, coaching his athletes to have faith in the unseen spirit.

Cerutty used to meet with his athletes around a campfire where he would speak of many of the great people in history and the common traits they shared, challenging his athletes with the responsibility they have of using their abilities to become the best they could be. Running, to Cerutty, was more than having the body run faster and faster. It was deeper than the confidence in the athlete's mind. Running to him was more about self-discovery—the recognition of one's own character or one's deepest spiritual reservoir. Here, while listening to my high-school idol, Herb Elliot, was another great inspirational message for me from another great coach!

Personal bests are exciting and rewarding, even more so I believe than receiving external accolades. Several years ago, I was asked to recall my most memorable moment from my experience with running, both as a runner and as a coach. It did not take me long to identify an evening in Novem-

31

ber 1959 after my high school junior year in cross country. I went alone in the dark of night to the outdoor track in Morton and used my father's stopwatch to time myself for a mile around the track. I still treasure that stopwatch and keep it in a drawer in my office. I was running a mile to see if I could get a personal best at a distance in which I had never broken five minutes.

There were no fans, no lights, no trophies, no medals, and no officials. It was just me, alone in the darkness, with my dad's stopwatch in my hand. My time of 4:58.6 marked one of the most satisfying moments of my competitive career—at the time it was my personal best!

Yet what was more important about my solo evening race: the time I had run, or the kind of person I became through the process I followed to run the time? The toughest competitor you will face in life is yourself. And the greatest satisfaction you can feel through running is the feeling of working toward a goal, reaching it, and knowing you have learned and absorbed the enduring values and attributes that have led you there.

These same responses to success are available to all young people who will work patiently to pursue a personal goal. You must fight your doubts and bounce back from your setbacks, believing in yourself and the value of your goal. Build your momentum with baby steps, by reaching one personal best after another. One doesn't climb a mountain by leaping to the top, but by patiently putting one foot in front of another, and sometimes working your way downhill to find a smarter path to ascend. And don't forget to seek out positive, like-minded people—your team—to accompany you on your journey. You will hear a lot in this book about the tremendous value of the people who might be your life's teammates.

When your goals are high, and are intrinsic, it takes time, work, and patience to reach them. Set reasonable goals for yourself to achieve today, this week, and next month, and pause to celebrate every goal you accomplish. Each will be your personal best performance so far! This is a recipe for personal growth and success that has worked very well for our North Central athletes spanning 50 years. It might well lead you to your personal success too.

CHAPTER 2

Purpose

"To be effective in initiating personal growth—
progressing toward one's goals—it is imperative that the
goals are personally and deeply felt."

–Coach Al Carius

"He who has a 'why' to live can bear almost any 'how.'"

–Friedrich Nietzsche

Running is very simple, and yet continuously complicated. At times I believe we have made running far too
scientific, complex, and materialistic in our country,
with very specific workouts intricately designed and tai-
lored for our individuals and teams. Fun, satisfaction, and
simplicity are a few keys to our success at North Central.

Through this lens, I respect Toby Tanser, who has
spent time in Kenya, explored Kenya, and complimented
the Kenyans for conserving joy and excitement in running. "We in the West have taken the most organic and
simple sport and turned it into the most overanalyzed
and overcomplicated thing." [*Lessons from the World's
Best Runners* by Duncan Larkin] Toby's main point about
running: "Keep it simple."

Speaking for simplicity, one of my All-American distance runners, Brian Wilson, once suggested an idea: "Coach, I have figured out how to beat the Kenyans." Curious, I answered, "How?" He responded, "By building them tracks and sending some of our coaches over there."

The key concept is simply "simplicity." Too many rules restrict the coach's and the program's flexibility to adapt to the external realities of today's society. "If we are not careful, we will out-policy ourselves!" This is how Coach Rob Harvey, one of our All-American runners and now a "Hall of Fame" high school coach himself, put it when discussing how complex some running programs have become in the US.

It amazes me how many books, articles, magazines, and clinics have been devoted to answering the questions surrounding achievement. At times it is confusing and overwhelming with the numerous gadgets and products that have been promoted to improve performance. It is ironic how complicated and overanalyzed we seem to have made such a pure and wholesome natural activity as running. We've taken something that is necessarily physically demanding, and hoped to reduce it into something "easy," aided by specialized shoes, wind-reducing clothing, special diets, and "magic" workout formulas. I have promoted one philosophy at North Central College for the past 50 years, and it is exciting to witness the fact that runners who understand and practice this simple "formula" are the ones who are most rewarded in the end.

Certainly, understanding the concepts of training and the science behind the workouts are important, yet I feel we too often bypass the most important key to success. It seems to me the key is not so much *what* we are doing in our training. It's rather finding inspiration to help the athletes to *want* to do the workout in the first place, and to maintain a lasting commitment to the daily steps in the preparation to reaching their goals. I tell my team each year that every freshman starts with great anticipation for his college experience, every distance runner begins the season with excitement, and each competition in a race feels good at the start. But how many of these people that start do all the little things daily that will lead them to their finish line? "Starting strong is good. Finishing strong is epic," as Canadian writer Robin Sharma wrote.

The real challenge begins after the start of school, or the season, or a race, when distractions, adversity, and disappointment become a part of the process. Joe Newton, the legendary coach from York High School in Elmhurst, Illinois, once told me that of all the high school runners, only 3% will continue to run in college and of that 3%, only 1% will continue to run during their senior year. He also said, "Successful people do what unsuccessful people will not do." So, commitment and persistence in pursuit of your goal is key. Maintaining the *fun* in the process while diligently pursuing your goal is like, well, like the spoonful of sugar that helps the medicine go down.

Simplicity, an appropriate lifestyle, and proper training are important principles within our track and cross country program. But where does the path begin for those who start our program, and hope to maintain their passion to finish their life's race? Each year during the first meeting with our freshmen runners, I explain two of the most important concepts of all. First, I explain that the sport does not care about what year in school you are. So don't limit yourself, or your belief in your abilities, with the label "freshman." Then, I focus their attention on the catalyst that initiates their journey with increased momentum—"What is their 'why'?"

To get their attention, I ask all the freshmen to stand up. I then begin an exaggerated and enthusiastic lecture suggesting that they should all immediately go to Tremont, Illinois. (Though, clearly, I know none of these athletes have even heard of Tremont nor know any route to get there.) I inform them that great advantages await them in Tremont when they arrive at this destination. I assure them that the coaches know the direction and every short cut route to get to this location. I tell them we can help them to attain these benefits in Tremont because of our experience and because we are passionate about directing each one of them. Our coaches are here to serve them.

For several minutes, I have them standing while I expand about how enthusiastic I am about making the journey with them and how supportive our coaching staff will be in planning and facilitating the details of their trip. "Our goal is for you to go to Tremont, Illinois," I tell the students. Throughout my presentation, a growing look of bewilderment is evident on the faces of our new freshmen class of runners. Beyond that, I am certain some may be questioning their choice of North Central College as well as the emotional stability of their new coach. After all, none of this initial speech seems to have any relevance to running. Finally, I stop ranting and ask them if any of them has any questions. I wait for the inevitable question and the freshman bold enough to ask it: "Why? Why would I want to go to Tremont, Illinois?"

This is the question and the answer I am waiting for. The depth of the athlete's passion in his answer will determine how rapidly and how far a person will progress in running, throwing, or jumping at North Central College. For that matter, it will influence if they even want to begin the journey. My point, of course, is not about getting to Tremont. It's about testing each athlete's self-knowledge of the "whys." Why are they running? Why are they running at North Central instead of another college? Why do they want to be the best runner they can be? And why might they agree to follow the lead of our veteran runners and our coaches? Unless each person can answer the "why" in their life, they cannot know their purpose. Without purpose, there is not intrinsic motivation. Without self-motivation, basically, there is little passion or little energy and therefore the "how" becomes insignificant. *Without intrinsic motivation, it does not matter what one's goals are.* To be effective in initiating self growth—progressing toward one's goals—it is imperative that an athlete's goals are personally established and deeply felt. Only then will their pursuit, guided by their "why" and driven by intrinsic motivation, be effective and lasting. Mark Twain put it succinctly: "The two most important days in your life are the day you are born and the day you find out why."

Goals are vitally important but, in my opinion, a coach should not give his athletes their goals. A coach can only reinforce and support the goals which the athlete intrinsically brings with him to the coach and the program. Nor can a coach really motivate an athlete either. He or she cannot force motivation but can only energize and nurture what the athlete chooses to do. I mistakenly used to think that I was a great motivator. With time, I have come to the conclusion that I can only supplement what a person has chosen to do in his heart.

In the 1970s, I read of the great power of intrinsic purpose, coming from a personal and deeply felt goal, on the subconscious mind. In Dr. Maxwell Maltz's book,

Psycho-Cybernetics, Maltz states that an instinctive goal-seeking "servo-mechanism" exists within each of us. This success mechanism subconsciously directs our conscious mind automatically toward our desired goal *if* the goal is self-generated deep within us—if it is intrinsic. In other words, when this servo-mechanism is at work for us, we do not need to stress, agonize, psych up, or force the process toward our goal. This is already taking place unconsciously, without stress or any external pressure, guiding us to facilitate a successful outcome.

One's pure intrinsic goal will be pursued with a focused, unconscious energy, according to Dr. Maltz. Essentially, one reaps whatever one sows with their thoughts and desires. "It is our attitude at the beginning of a difficult task," wrote William James, "which, more than anything else, will affect its successful outcome." I believe that Dr. Maltz is the father of modern sports psychology, and his work inspired my coaching.

Interesting thing, according to Maltz, this success mechanism already exists within each of us and is triggered automatically when the goal set is personally intrinsic. Ironically, this mechanism is often negated when an athlete or team consciously tries too hard to reach this goal. Each of us has a "sweet spot" on our emotional performance curve. We have to find it through trial and error. Our positive expectations provide us with energy to enhance the effort toward the best outcome.

But too much emotion may take an athlete over the peak of his emotional performance curve. "Trying too hard" to reach a goal sends too many nervous impulses to too many muscle fibers, causing a tightening or tension which can interfere physically with the progress toward the goal. It's a kind of paralysis through over-analysis. One should "Let it happen rather than make it happen." The athlete must allow his subconscious mind to guide his internal muscle memory toward his goal in a relaxed, reflexive, mechanically efficient flow. You cannot force this process during a race or other athletic performance. Permit your "success mechanism" to pilot the process to your goal.

Here's an example that might better explain what I'm talking about. Consider a child learning to walk. It's a complicated process that takes the child months and hundreds of falls and missteps. The child, unknowing, must first "learn" the feeling of sending the correct number of nervous impulses to the appropriate muscle fibers to develop the muscle memory to take each step toward a goal. But, once the child develops that muscle memory, he no longer has to "think through" or struggle with each step. He walks automatically, reflexively, intuitively, without thinking. He has "learned" to walk, and (barring injury) will know how to do it the rest of his life. Just like learning to ride a bike. Inherently, he is allowing his "success mechanism" to guide the process of walking without outside interference.

Even for a child, it's a natural development. It operates at the subconscious level and Dr. Maltz called it the "servo-mechanism." It becomes a reflexive, effortless process of letting happen what the body has already learned to do through repetitive practice. This harmony between the nervous system and the body is called "kinesthetic science." Your body has learned the action, so you do not need to "make" it happen with your mind. You just "let" it happen. Like in a game of ping pong, after months or years of playing, you don't think about every shot. You just act reflexively in the present.

As adults and as athletes, we call it "being in the now," in the moment, in the zone, in a groove, or in the flow. If you've done the necessary work, run the miles, thrown the throws, practiced the piano, learned your lines, on the day of your performance your body will know what to do through muscle memory. The preparation has to be yours, and the goal needs to be yours too, so that you'll have the self-motivation to carry you through the obstacles between you and your goal.

As I said, I used to believe I could motivate athletes, but now realize that I can only reinforce what an athlete or team chooses to do as intuitively felt by them through their personal goals. Without the "why" answered, extrinsic "pep talks" are of little lasting value while running in cold, heat, wind, rain, snow, dark, during two-a-day workouts, or on long runs. Such talks are merely empty external words, if they're not accompanied by the athlete's own deeper commitment, and therefore will not initiate their servo-mechanism. Ted Haydon once told me of a champion runner he knew whose primary workout was repeat 100s on a football field. He also told me, "If you have an athlete who is motivated, you can have him do almost anything in a workout, and he will get better and improve. If you have an athlete who is not motivated, you can do almost anything in a workout, and he will not get better and will not improve."

A coach's responsibility is to keep the culture and environment as supportive, positive, and clear of outside interference as possible to allow the athletes and team to focus on their passion and thoughts to pursue their goals. This reminds me of the Biblical passage spoken by Jesus about the sowing of seeds. I enjoy working in my yard and rearranging plants and flowers as part of my energy recharging process when not teaching or coaching. I refer to our athletes as seeds that must be planted in rich soil (culture), and given appropriate amounts of water, sunlight, and fertilizer while also keeping the weeds out. If you have the right seeds and control the environment, the plants will naturally grow to their fullest potential. Again, the coach's responsibility is to find the best seeds, control the environment, and guide them along the path that the athlete and the team have chosen in route to their goals.

Our program is based upon finding the right athletes, with readiness of purpose, who have answered their "why" concerning running, jumping, or throwing, and bring self-motivation to each practice. We reinforce athletes who look for what they can get from each practice to help them grow, who say, "What do I *get* to do today?" rather than "What do we *have* to do today?" This is a clear benefit of coaching Division III athletes at North Central, who do not get paid for participating but run and throw and jump for the love of the sport.

Our system at North Central is uncomplicated, but requires a thorough understanding of its concepts: strong intrinsic motivation, devotion to a good work ethic, a sense of perspective and a desire to have fun, a commitment to goals—and the discipline to pursue them. Discipline is the mental toughness—the *self*-discipline—to do the right things day after day. We have learned over time that, "A lack of self-discipline in one area of your life can often carry over to other areas of your life." I don't know who originally said that but, as a coach, I have seen it is true.

Training boils down to basic physiology. Distance runners run faster times by improving the efficiency of the body to sustain greater speeds over longer periods of time past

40 meters. That ability is improved by gradually enhancing the body's ability to transport oxygen and nutrients to the tissues and to rid the body of the waste products associated with exercise. This concept of physiology is well known and documented. I was first introduced to "educational of the physical" with an exercise physiology course in the 1960s at the University of Illinois by the world famous Tom Cureton. Dr. Cureton established the first adult fitness program in the world. By understanding the concept objective, the runner opens up numerous pathways for himself to meet the objective in a more holistic, individualized way.

Nearly everyone can take advantage of the benefits of running and see his or her times improve through the positive physiological adaptations of training, with just the patience to allow it to work in a gradual, progressive way. Any runner can enjoy the rewards. No coach's decision can keep someone from participating, no official can affect a runner's performance, and few physical limitations can hold a determined runner back.

I have seen many runners and track and field athletes with seemingly modest athletic ability gradually improve to the point of becoming outstanding distance runners, throwers, jumpers, and sprinters. One of our very best, six-time NCAA Division III National Champion Dan Mayer, provides a great example of that. Mayer did not have top accolades coming out of high school in New Holstein, Wisconsin. But in 1994, Mayer's times in the 10,000-meter and 5,000-meter races would have won the Division I titles for those events in that year. In 1996, he posted America's fourth best 10,000-meter time of 28:19 as he qualified for the Olympic trials in Atlanta, Georgia. Again, he qualified for the trials in the marathon in 2000.

Another example is Justin Rapp, a thrower from our local Wheaton North High School, where his best throw with the 12-pound high school shot was 50 feet. After one year at North Central, he sat down with our long-time throws coach, Pat Gora, and another of our great throwers, Adam Moody, from Naperville North. Both young throwers discussed with Gora their desire to become a national champion in their sport. Mentally, they set that goal for themselves then and there, while Gora helped them lay out a training plan to pursue to meet those goals.

"They believed it," Coach Gora reminded me recently. "They started listening to my coaching and worked really hard over the next few years to reach their goals." With his work and his focused effort, Adam Moody placed 3rd in the Division III nationals twice. And Justin Rapp? He ended his career at North Central with the throw of his career, tossing the larger 16-pound college-level shot an astounding 56 feet, 5 and 1/4 inches. And he threw that personal best throw on the last toss of his career, at nationals, and became the NCAA Division III National Champion in the shot in 2002. See what a young man can do when he sets a personal goal for himself, and pursues it to the best of his ability?

Jeff Hansen is another unforgettable example of an athlete who traveled the path of purpose after discovering his "why," resulting in a tremendous unleashing of personal growth. Hansen entered NCC as a freshman with untapped ability and uncommitted attitude. However, I remember the exact spot in outdoor track at the Lewis University steeplechase pit when he had his "ah ha" moment on ending his first-year collegiate experience. He communicated, very determinedly, "Next year I am going to come back in shape!" In other words, Hansen answered his "why" and found his purpose—setting in motion his servo-mechanism. Hansen made a commitment for what he wanted to do—perform at his best.

Throughout his remaining three years at North Central College, while there were good days and not so good, ups and downs, celebrations and disappointments, Jeff remained steadfast in that commitment he made at that defining moment at the steeplechase pit. Patient, disciplined, and intrinsically motivated, his steady growth is reflected through his times. As a freshman, Hansen had a personal best of 17:39 in the 5,000 meters. As a senior, he dropped his time to 14:37, placing him third in the NCAA Indoor Championships held at Illinois Wesleyan University.

Realistically, all of these athletes had to do their own work over time to improve their performances and make the effort to reach their goals. But they were not alone during the process. Besides having the support of their team members, they've received wonderful advice and guidance from our amazing group of assistant coaches, volunteer and paid, at North Central College during my 50+ years of coaching. I can never mention them all individually— though I have tried to list as many as I can remember at the back of this book. But I thank and congratulate them all collectively, for this head coach and his athletes would never have achieved the performances I celebrate here without the work and support of my assistant coaches over the years.

Tim Winder, our pole vault coach, like Pat Gora, is another great example of the dedicated, thoughtful, and talented coaches who have guided our athletes over the years. Winder's own sons, Jake, Josh, and Luke were all outstanding pole vaulters while at North Central. Amazingly, each of them became a Division III National Champion in the event, and they seemed to take brotherly pride in out-performing each other by setting one NCC school vaulting record after another. However, Winder recalled for me the performances of another of his vaulters, Steve Stack, who set personal best after personal best while at North Central.

Stack came to North Central with a modest high school best in the pole vault of 12 feet. But he was a hard worker, quickly bought into the philosophy of our program, and blossomed. Guided by Winder, Stack didn't concentrate on just his technical execution while vaulting. He focused on how to work, how to conduct himself, and how to have faith—in himself, his coach, and our program. He kept plugging away at his sport, and frankly saved himself a lot of time on the learning curve by following the guidance of his coaches. In 2010, Stack qualified for Division III nationals his senior year with his last jump at our Last Chance meet before the national meet. He went on to become an All–American vaulter, 5th in the nation, with a personal best vault of 16 feet, 3 and 1/2 inches at nationals. From a 12-foot jump to more than 16 feet! Steve Stack showed us how to climb that mountain toward personal goals, one step at a time.

Coach Winder reminded me, when retelling this story, that what makes these victories so valuable for athletes like Steve Stack is the struggle they go through to achieve them. They learn to set goals, think for themselves, work through the process, and be men. Stack, like hundreds of our athletes, became a coach himself—head coach at Naperville Central high school—and is guiding other athletes in his turn. You can view a list of our NCC athletes-turned-coaches at the back of this book.

Numerous others have had similar stories. Tony Bleull, from tiny Putnam County High School in central Illinois, ran 28:05 for 8,000 meters his freshman year to place 189th in the NCAA Cross Country Championships held in Rochester, New York. Tony went on, after 3 years of dedication and hard work, to become the Division III NCAA National Champion in 1983 while setting a national record of 23:46 at the course in Newport, Virginia. John Collet, who could not break 63 seconds in the 400 meters and had a nickname of "Crash Collet" because of the frequency that he fell down while running and walking, came to North Central College with a best performance of 21st place in his conference cross country championships. Collet, following his "why," still went on to be a five-time All-American at North Central in cross country and track. Dan Kerley, a 10:42 high-school two-miler, and Roger Klein (10:24) both progressed to run a sub-30-minute 10,000 meters and became repeat All-Americans.

These are but a few of the many examples of athletes answering their "why" among our 800+ All-Americans, and the countless personal bests within our program. Parents and athletes often ask what kind of performances or times they need from high school to become a part of our program. The answer is that we do not evaluate entrance onto the team by previous performance or statistics but rather by passion, character, and especially attitude, just like Ted Haydon did. Anyone who loves to compete and has a passion to improve, regardless of his high school performances, is welcomed to our team and, through this mindset, will make positive contributions to the flow of synergistic energy supporting the culture of North Central College cross country and track & field.

In contrast to those who answer the question "why" and understand the concepts with purpose, I have also sadly seen those with great potential who never found their "why" to running, throwing, or jumping at the collegiate level, and who never really connected with and absorbed our philosophy. Fortunately, this is a choice that athletes have in a non-scholarship athletic program like North Central's. In other words, I should say these individuals never really felt it within. They didn't adopt the deep internal glue uniting the mind, body, and spirit, into a lifestyle leading to personal-best success. They didn't succeed in connecting their training with their servo-mechanism. Perhaps they did not see or choose the right path within our program.

Instead, these runners with great potential became one of the many seasonal athletes—ignoring that there are 365 days a year available to all of us to personally grow and to maximize our God-given abilities. Some show a superficial excitement about running at the beginning of a career or season, but, human nature being what it is, they want immediate results or lack the intrinsic desire to overcome the many challenging difficulties along the way. It is not uncommon among athletes to be drawn toward the external authority of a multitude of cultural trends and youthful distractions that keep them from focusing on day-by-day consistency in the training process. Indiana Coach Bobby Knight described the problem succinctly: "Your biggest opponent isn't the other guys. It's human nature."

There are many trials and much adversity faced in the daily process of working toward a personal goal, since the path is not straightforward. It has been stated that a runner must learn the difference between good fatigue and bad fatigue. He must learn the difference between soreness and an injury, and the difference between pain and discomfort. But even coupled with the best of intentions, enthusiasm without patience, diligence, and purpose can lead to a "too soon, too much, too fast" impatient approach. This may lead to injured muscles for athletes and frustrating disappointment for anyone pursuing their life's goal. A key principle to adopt is "delayed gratification." The servo–mechanism itself is a tremendous tool to help an injured athlete navigate with the needed perseverance through the adversity of an injury. It has been said that there are three ways to respond to an injury or adversity. One: quit. Two: allow the injury to heal and then repeat the same lifestyle or pattern of behavior that led to the injury in the first place. And three: Learn from the injury, and change the pattern and path that led to the injury in the first place.

Jerry Ashmore was an All-American from Western Michigan University. He and I were warming up one day before a track meet while representing the University of Chicago Track Club. He put the importance of the internal strength of one's personal servo-mechanism in perspective by saying, "You know Al, there are more tough days in running than great days." Another UCTC athlete, Rick Wohlhuter—the Olympic Bronze medalist in the 800 meters in 1976 and former world record holder at 880 yards and 1000 meters—noted, "You must experience failure and defeat many times before you reach the top." Or, before you fully learn how to make the most of your God-given talents.

Each day is an adventure and a hunt to find and absorb the benefits of the challenges along that path. You must have great persistence, discipline, and mental toughness to overcome those hard days and the adversity that will be part of the process of pursuing your goals, in running, in track & field, and in life. NBA basketball great Jerry West noted, "You can't get much done in life if you only work on days when you feel good."

Keep your eyes on the prize, but your feet on the roads. Serious improvement in their college athletic performances is nearly impossible for seasonal runners. But any runner can share in the intrinsic rewards found in Tremont, Illinois. Give your training purpose. Make it a lifestyle. Remain focused, patient, gradual, and consistent, and study the concepts taught by your coach. Be open, with faith in the unseen, to the educational values learned through experience in a track & field or a cross country program. But first you, the athlete, must answer your "why" question.

CHAPTER 3

Academics and Athletics

"The importance of sport is not winning but redefining continually what success and failure are. It is the ongoing personal exploration, not of the narrow limitations of the body, but of the boundless spirit trapped within."

—Eric Thornton, NCC running alumnus, 1966

"We focus rather on education through the physical, on development of character along with the science, which leads to self-growth and self-mastery."

—Coach Al Carius

In 1973, I was asked to speak at a track and cross country coaches clinic at University of Wisconsin–Stevens Point. Better than that, imagine my surprise when it gave me the opportunity to meet and talk to the great Jesse Owens, who was the real highlight for me.

Owens, of course, is a true inspiration for any track athlete or coach, and certainly was for me. He won 4 gold medals at the 1936 Berlin Olympics and held the world long jump record for 25 years. In one college meet in 1935, he broke three world records and tied a fourth—in one day. Talk about personal bests!

But far more important, Jesse Owens was a role model for the world to learn from. "Being a role model," Coach John Wooden wrote, "is the most powerful form of educating."

During my session of the clinic, I spoke very little of the physical science of our workouts at North Central College. I felt the physiology of training was well known at the time and that a "cookie cutter" training plan for all would not be in the coaches' best interest, as they pursued better performances from their teams.

What was becoming obvious to me from coaching at North Central was that the *process* that leads to personal bests was a deeper, more powerful force, originating at an expanded, invisible level, than simply the physical workouts themselves. Although very difficult to explain, this unseen force magnified the known science of the physiology of workouts to elevated levels. I was discovering a non-physical truth moving performances to a new level.

Success is not one-dimensional and not everyone can achieve the same result from a standard workout applied to an athlete on a team. Again, running physiology is well known, but the path leading to full potential is complex and complicated by adversity and numerous challenges along the way. What really mattered to me, and what I honestly wanted to talk about, was our running philosophy. I hoped to go beyond the mere discussion of the physical aspects of running and speak of the immeasurable influences, on athletes and on teams, about which there was little research and few concrete answers. My topic for the clinic was "The strength and inner power of intrinsic motivation in contrast with extrinsic motivation." I wanted to share some of the wisdom, beyond the physical, I had learned from Dr. Maxwell Maltz. I hoped to relate it to distance running for the coaches present.

Inspired by this topic, I was more passionate in my Stevens Point talk about the opportunities that distance running provides to athletes to make personal choices for furthering their goals. Throughout their journey, athletes must decide what personal path they will follow, what they can say "Yes" to, and what they must say "No" to, with each choice leading them toward their inner-directed growth and maturity. The opportunities are numerous and the choices important for self-discovery.

Years ago, in the old *Chicago Daily News,* the columnist Sydney J. Harris expressed this importance: "Ninety percent of the world's woe comes from people not knowing themselves, their abilities, their frailties, and even their real virtues. Most of us go almost all the way through life as complete strangers to ourselves—so how can we know anyone else?"

Our program at its best helps to escort the athlete toward the depths of their gifts that cannot be measured by science, but will ultimately translate into helping him become the best he is capable of being in life. My goal for our athletes at North Central College is not about outcome, but about maximizing their God-given talent during the process.

This definition of success is again a reflection and a tribute to my mentor, Ted Haydon. Ted's aura and rare spirit, even in the briefest encounters, made every person feel that they already occupied a significant place in Ted's heart, and that Ted understood the person holistically, accepting him as a unique individual, and would champion him as a friend. Ted showed me the way. I learned from him not to emphasize results but rather the needs and well-being of my individual athletes.

After the clinic was over, I received feedback from my Assistant Coach Glenn Behnke whose brother, Donn

Behnke, was in attendance. Donn is a highly successful high school coach in Wisconsin, and author of the excellent cross country memoir, *The Animal Keepers*. Donn told Glenn that my speech was not favorably received by the coaches around him, but that the athletes in attendance enjoyed the presentation. Somewhat amazingly, as I was finishing up this book, Donn wrote me a letter reminding me of *his* view of my talk that day from the perspective of a young athlete, and the lifelong effects it had on him as a runner and a coach.

> *Dear Al. You may not remember this, but in the winter of 1973 you spoke at a coaching clinic in Stevens Point, Wisconsin. I was a sophomore at UWSP at the time and incredibly frustrated with the coaching I'd received up to that point in my college running career. In the finest Behnke tradition I found a way to sneak into the clinic (without paying of course) in hopes of learning the secret of Al Carius and the guys at North Central.*
>
> *With notebook in hand I found a seat in the front of the room and prepared to write down every last thing you had to say. Like everyone else I was expecting a barrage of numbers and a precise, detailed, day by day listing of the exact workouts guaranteed to produce great runners. We all wanted the Al Carius secret formula: something we could condense down to a 3x5 inch notecard and follow like one of grandma's favorite recipes. We were searching for something simple and foolproof, a sort of "paint by numbers" approach to coaching. But as you know, that's not at all what you gave us.*

What you gave us was something far better and exactly what I needed to hear at that point in my running career. You talked about methods and forms of motivation along with the value of commitment, self-discipline, personal responsibility, and goal setting. You explained how you went about building a team, how you treated your runners, and how you built relationships with them. While the lack of mention of workouts or mileage totals was a source of great frustration to the two ** coaches who sat behind me, I want you to know that I was profoundly and positively changed by listening to you that day. I listened intently and didn't take a single note, I didn't need to. I captured much of it, held onto it, adapted it to my own situation, and have thought back on it many times in my coaching career.

Thank you for being such a good role model and positive influence on me, even if it was in a rather strange and round-about way. Most of what I know about running and coaching came to me through you, the North Central program, and of course my brother Glenn...

Unlike young Donn Behnke, the coaches that day wanted to hear about the science of the physical aspects of our workouts at North Central. This response, in contrast to what I most enjoy speaking about, has been fairly common whenever I have been asked to speak before a group of coaches. If I begin the presentation asking if there are any questions, invariably the first questions relate to the workouts at North Central College and the specifics relating to them. Their focus is on the physical, while I am most passionate to talk about working through the physical to help the student-athlete learn and grow beyond the physical.

Again, running physiology is simple and yet performance is very complex on the path to an athlete's self-mastery and success. Too often we look to the tangible, uncomplicated explanation to describe making the most of our God-given talents. We are being bombarded with one-dimensional solutions for results that, in my opinion, require a more holistic, interconnected approach. Even in Division III colleges, we are too often not pursuing the most important goal: the educational purpose and life-long benefits for athletes from participation in a sports program.

There was a time in the early 1980s after we had won four NCAA Division III national cross country titles, (1975, 1976, 1978, and 1979), that three men appeared at my door in North Central's Merner Fieldhouse. They had heard that our cross country team had meetings around a spring-fed pond in front of Merner Fieldhouse. At this time, the spring bubbled water from the ground and flowed down a stream leading to the pond. They asked if our team drank from the spring during our gatherings. I indicated that occasionally we did drink the spring water. Again, looking for a narrow, simple, tangible scientific explanation for our success, they asked to test the water to see if there were any hidden performance ingredients that could be measured!

Apparently, these men hoped to scientifically reveal a singular, rational, external property of the water that enhanced our team's performances. Needless to say, nothing unique or magical was found within the spring water by these three men. This was not surprising but yet another example of looking to measurable science to explain something that, when at our best, can only truly be completely understood with faith *internally*. Instead of merely focusing on the short-term training *of* the body, with tangible science, we focus rather on education *through* the body, on the development of character complimenting the physiology, which leads to more significant self-mastery.

For me and for our program, I have come to know that the greatest value from participating on a cross country or a track & field team and being a runner/thrower/jumper is the constant struggle of the athlete against himself as he works his way to the finish line. During a cross country race, you learn there is no straight path to the finish, and adversity will be a part of the process. Interestingly, I was going through some papers at home and came across a quote which I believe continues to capture a core element of our program. Eric Thornton, one of my former runners who competed at North Central College in my first year (1966), wrote this in 1987: "The importance of sport is not winning but redefining continually what success and failure are. It is the ongoing personal exploration, not of the narrow limitations of the body, but of the boundless spirit trapped within."

Cross country races are not easy and are filled with countless external and internal challenges, including rough course terrain and bad weather. Regarding these challenges, Nike founder and legendary University of Oregon coach Bill Bowerman once stated, "There is no such thing as bad weather, just weak people." I myself have said, "The worse the conditions, the more advantage to the best-prepared teams who have inner confidence."

In the years when we know that our teams are well prepared, we regularly tell them that the more challenging the external conditions, the greater advantage we have. Those without this authentic confidence may subconsciously give themselves an excuse when the going gets tough. During the middle and the final stages of a race, their preconceived evaluation of the race conditions may have a negative effect subconsciously on their whole race experience. Poor conditions help to separate the great from the good during competition. Calvin College's runners certainly showed this at the muddy, rain-soaked national championship meet in 2006, when they ran away from the field despite the horrible course conditions.

It may come as a shock to some that adversity can create a long-term advantage for us. In spite of the challenges it presents to runners, adversity can contribute to the development of core resilience skills to help us cope with life's challenges. To this point, Sydney Harris also wrote, "Life is nine-tenths a matter of learning to cope. If you do not learn to cope with the little things, the big things will overwhelm you." Ironically, one of the many benefits of sport is the challenge of difficulties experienced along the way to the athlete's goal, and his subsequent response to the strain of the stress. "The greatest weapon against stress," noted William James, "is our ability to choose one thought over another." Forced to choose, to fight the difficulties and the stress, we are encouraged to grow.

When I was young, teachers often spoke about the importance of intellectual intelligence (IQ) as the key to future success. Over time, more and more people began to recognize the more influential significance of emotional intelligence (EQ) as a stronger indication for achievement. It has been reported that 85% of success is attributed to a person's attitude and only 15% to their knowledge, a strong endorsement of emotional intelligence.

More recently, Dr. Paul Stoltz has written about the relevance of one's adversity quotient, or AQ, and its added influence on future success. For example, he relates that one's AQ is how a person responds to life, especially the tough challenges along the way. "The stronger your AQ," Dr. Stoltz reported, "the more effectively you will respond to adversity and the less life's events will take a toll on your energy, performance, health and outlook."

I must admit I am sometimes concerned that too many of today's youth are being encouraged to grow more "mature" with knowledge but are less mature emotionally, and do not have the necessary internal coping skills or mechanisms to deal with life's increasing complex challenges. Too many are turning to external distractions as a means to deflect their stress and pain. The inability to deal effectively with stress is becoming a bigger and more widespread problem with too many of our younger generation. Alcohol and drug use, cutting, depression, and unfortunately, even suicide are on the increase.

Life is difficult—running is difficult. In coaching, there is a major difference between "spoon-feeding" and nurturing. And there is a considerable distinction between pampering and allowing for maturing through inherent setbacks.

Recently, in our local *Daily Herald* newspaper, I read an article "Why Teens Need Strong Coping Skills." Gena Bogen, a social worker at Waubonsie Valley High School, was quoted in the article. "When we don't let our children fail, when we don't give them a chance to not be first, we don't allow them to build those skills they need to be resilient. It is important that children learn that failure isn't the end of the world. Sometimes we have to let them feel the pain so they know they will survive."

So, as improbable as it may seem at times, early exposure to losing and failure has advantages for a young person in discovering how to cope with disappointment and the stress all our youth encounter as a part of life as they struggle to grow up. Again, my mentor Ted Haydon regularly said of our University of Chicago Track Club dual meets against Division I programs, "It is to our advantage to lose, because if we win we will not be invited back again by many of the Division I schools, which have primarily outcome-oriented programs that focus on places, points, and winning. Our Track Club members will lose the opportunity to do what they love to do—compete." Even our young people can "win in losing"—but more on that later.

Coach Haydon always knew that the most important thing was not in the winning but in the opportunity for athletes to learn and grow through their involvement in sport. Oddly enough, in the long run it really is not the outcome that is most important but rather the life lessons and wisdom acquired through the doing that matters most. Regardless of the outcome, the athlete benefits from the opportunity to release and strengthen the survival "spirit" trapped within. This is why, at North Central, we feel so strongly that athletics is a fundamental supplement to academics. It is not merely an extracurricular activity, but is rather a firmer foundation on which students can decide to transform personal weaknesses into strengths.

An athlete's final time and place in any race are but a reflection of the personal growth experienced in the process. Coaches, like teachers with students, help to spark the flame and escort the athlete in a direction to absorb the many life lessons of the journey. Sydney J. Harris explained the purpose of teaching this way: "At the highest level, the purpose of teaching is not to teach. It is to inspire the desire for learning. Once a student's mind is on fire, it will find a way to provide its own fuel." I feel the same way about coaching, and athletics. We work to inspire the fire within our student-athletes. When we succeed, we get to watch the momentum build as they approach the potentials of their God-given talents.

Running a race, and life, are each a journey full of the history lived and people met along the way, with the support and guidance of a mentor coach or coaches, that provide a spiritual flow to feed our soul's growth. Life is not lived in a daily straight line, smoothly traveled, without numerous challenges, hazards, emotional turmoil, and adversity along the way. Adversity is inevitable for each of us along the ever-winding path of our life. Every morning now, I walk by a sign in a car window that gives us great advice: "Be kinder than necessary because everyone you meet is fighting some kind of battle." [J. M. Barrie]

Our inner strength and focused discipline, exemplified by our spirit, provides the servo-mechanism (described by Dr. Maxwell Maltz) for us to continue to press on toward our finish line. Cross country and track & field provide an ideal environmental platform for the unseen influence of spiritual growth to feed our souls, to help us come to know what we believe, to live life in harmony with those beliefs, and to let our soul shine for others. Running—all athletics—provides an avenue to achieve this harmony within the educational exposure. How each race is run, and coming to know oneself, is far more important than who wins. "The self," John Dewey noted, "is not something ready made, but something in continuous formation through choice of action."

One of my biggest concerns about the present state of education is witnessing the slow separation between athletics and academics at the collegiate level. I have witnessed this slow detachment since my freshman year in the fall of 1960 at the University of Kansas. But why and how did we get to this place? Unfortunately, the drive for materialistic outcomes from participation in sports is increasingly creeping down from professional sports into all levels of athletic participation. At many levels, we have abandoned our focus on the holistic development of the student's mind, body, and spirit. Coaches, parents, and the athletes themselves are often focusing on—or being encouraged to concentrate on—what they can "get," monetarily, from being an athlete. "Train hard enough and you'll get a scholarship, Son!"

As a coach and a dad and a Grampa, when I hear this kind of comment, I want to cry out, "But where's the joy?! Aren't young people supposed to play sports for *fun*?" Is money really what we want our athletes to be striving for? In reality, only a tiny number of high school athletes get scholarships. An even smaller percentage of them make money as an athlete after college. Why would we encourage young people to pursue athletics for so crass a reason? Ninety-nine point nine percent of them will *fail* as an athlete if an athletic scholarship is their goal. But all of them have a great possibility to enjoy their sport, learn life lessons from it, and achieve individual success, if they are encouraged to pursue personal bests.

We must deal with the whole person and not just the externals of money, numbers, records, grades, statistics, and facts. Don't get me wrong: it is wonderful that some high school athletes get athletic scholarships that help them go to college. Many couldn't afford to attend otherwise. But athletics has broader benefits for young people, and I think we are wrong to focus their attentions excessively on the externals like money that only a very few of them will earn. Athletics provides, among many other good benefits, the opportunity to help young people learn to connect with their deep roots, and to relate with others. I believe this is one of the most pressing problems young people deal with today. It is reported that 70% of workers who lose their jobs do so not because they don't know their trade, but because they cannot relate and get along with others by blending selflessly into a group team environment.

Education at its best should help inspire and prepare a student for introspective growth throughout life. "Your perception will become clear," noted Carl Jung, "when you look into your soul." As a coach, I would like you to consider this: sports conducted within the proper atmosphere will contribute to that end. Furthermore, it seems to me there is at this time an unprecedented need for athletics to be recognized as a healthy avenue for character education, as curricular instead of extra-curricular. John Wooden once said, "A coach's primary function should be not to make better players but to make better people."

As far as I am concerned, there is an undercurrent in our increasingly complex cultural environment which in some cases is slowly eroding the foundation of our self, or who we are—our soul. Sadly, the line of distinction between right and wrong, good and bad, has narrowed. A few years ago, I was walking a recruit and his family through our recreation center where the Olympic women's basketball coach from DePaul University, Doug Bruno, was conducting a summer basketball clinic for girls. Doug spotted me and came over to say, "Hi."

I remember asking Doug what the difference was now in coaching young people in the new millennium compared to his early years of coaching. His answer was profound: "The youth of today are no different than the youth of the past. The difference is within our coaching ranks. Our job today should be to teach the student-athletes the absolute values and truths that were taught, absorbed, and lived by the people who helped make our country great. Those values that lead to success are the same today. It is our responsibility to teach these values to the youth of the current generation."

Coaches of character and a positive athletic experience can have a lasting positive influence in the education of the whole person, shaping tangible values of character like having a good work ethic, commitment, discipline, teamwork, loyalty, resilience, integrity, honesty, sportsmanship, and intrinsic motivation. These internal virtues are absolute, represent true lasting victories, and must be reinforced consistently. I will have much more to say later in this book about the fundamental importance of this job for a coach.

Too often I have seen athletes who relied solely on their natural talent while not developing their hidden internal gifts. In time, often, these talented athletes get passed in our meet lineups by less-physically-endowed runners whose focus on their inner virtues magnifies their physical powers. Sadly, the athlete with superior gifts and potential can unfortunately end up believing and rationalizing that he just "lacks sufficient talent." Throughout my long coaching career, I have given hundreds of recommendations to various businesses and agencies about former athletes. No one has ever requested the performance times, distances, or heights achieved by the athlete. The question is always about the athlete's character, or their unseen internal strengths. Athletics, at its best, is a means of recognizing and reinforcing those depths of eternal character. Carl Jung said it this way: "Who looks outside, dreams; who looks inside, awakes." When I attended the University of Illinois, I was fortunate to have taken courses taught by teacher-coaches. This being so, I had the opportunity to take a football class taught by Pete Elliot, who coached the Illini football team to a 17-7 victory over Washington in the 1964 Rose Bowl. Beyond that, a member of that Rose Bowl team and a fellow classmate was Dick Butkus, the future star of the Chicago Bears. I have a story or two to tell about him later in this book. During my four years of undergraduate studies at Illinois, I had several other courses taught by the head coaches of Illinois's varsity athletic teams. At the same time, I began even so long ago to see a division being created between the Athletic department and the Physical Education department, no longer linking athletics with academics. However, all the while I was there, the coaches in the Athletic department also taught academic classes within the University, linking athletics with academics. In my opinion, it has become a rarity now to find a coach who is also a teacher of an academic course.

When I began at North Central College, all coaches were hired to also teach in an academic program on campus. Sadly, in the age of specialization, coaches no longer teach at North Central College. Hence, I believe the gap between academics and athletics continues to grow wider and wider. I have always pictured myself as a teacher-coach. Early in my career, I was on a path to lead the University of Illinois Chicago Circle (now the University of Illinois at Chicago) Physical Education program's Foundation of Physical Education, in the spring of 1966 while pursuing my Masters degree. I never set out to be a coach but rather to be a teacher in the field of physical education and pursue my Doctorate in the Physiology of Exercise.

My concern is that this ongoing athletic/academic division continues to grow with the spread and expansion of travel teams and club teams for much younger children. Traditionally, those young athletes would be under the guidance of a school teacher-coach who is philosophically connected to the education mission and model. In addition, I am somewhat uneasy about our emphasis on standardized test scores to evaluate one's level of "education" in our school systems, rather than emphasizing the development of a student's character.

In too many ways, I feel we are draining from athletics and education the values of humanity which must be taught and recognized as a major part of the process. Instead of prioritizing these lasting life values, we too often overemphasize the outcomes—scores, grades, times, places, victories—of students' academic and athletic performances. I believe it is too easy for us—coaches and athletes and parents—to be focused mainly on what is tangible, and measurable by our five senses, at the expense of what is often more significant below (or above) the surface of the physical.

As a coach, I am often reminded of one of John Denver's songs, "Some Days are Diamonds." The lyrics have crossed my mind many times and have helped me to stay true to the fundamental core values of our motto: "Run for fun and personal bests."

Some days are diamonds, some days are stone
Sometimes the hard times won't leave me alone
Sometimes a cold wind blows a chill in my bones
Some days are diamonds, some days are stone
Now the face that I see in my mirror
More and more is a stranger to me
More and more I can see there's a danger
In becoming what I never thought I'd be

Whenever I hear Denver's lyrics, they remind me to resist the lures of the external, and reconnect with and reaffirm the core ideals which we must adhere to at North Central College. It is a coach's responsibility to protect the integrity of teaching through coaching the whole person—uniting mind, body, and spirit to lead students to self-discovery and ultimately self-mastery. I try to share with our athletes Emerson's reminder, "We gain the strength of the temptation we resist."

There are many outside influences drawing our young student-athletes in confusing or questionable directions when, or if, they themselves are not supported by absolute rock-solid moral platforms. In education and in athletics, we are in a constant battle for the hearts, minds, and spirit of those we influence on a daily basis, to lead them to this solid ground for personal development through participation. A fine guiding principle is found in a quote by Baron de Coubertin, the first president of the International Olympic Committee: "The most important thing in the Olympic Games is not to win but to take part. Just as the most important thing in life is not the triumph but the struggle. The essential thing is not to have conquered but to have fought well."

Phil Coleman, my distance coach at the University of Illinois, spoke profoundly about this years ago, "An amateur's commitment to sport is a qualified commitment, an acknowledgment that he will give his all only within certain restrictions. He will do his utmost in his two hours a day, knowing he might be better if he spent eight hours or if he added weightlifting or if he dropped spices from his diet or quit sleeping with his wife. He strives to do the utmost within his limits but has the reservation that if he is not himself victorious, this does not mean that he is defeated. Amateurism is a point of view, a state of mind. It is an attitude toward sport that recognizes it as something other than a profession, something other than life's work, something other than a livelihood or means of existence."

Coach Coleman's comments echo the sporting values that are supposed to underlie the quadrennial Olympic Games. The ancient Olympic Games were based upon standards of values, morals, and ideals including virtue, noble competition, honor, freedom, and peace. The competitions valued "moral rewards more than profit. An athlete exhibited restraint and avoided overzealous behavior. A noble competitor accepted both defeat and victory gracefully." For myself, I believe that the path taken by a team is primarily driven by the order and rank of traits of character they choose to follow.

My experiences with, and the influence of, coaches Phil Coleman and Ted Haydon have had a lasting positive effect on my coaching and my life. Sport for me has always been about the positive values it has taught—a part of my life but never my entire life. I remind our athletes daily when they cross our "red line of balance" coming into our locker room. On their way to practice, the line reminds them to focus and to be the best athlete and teammate they can be. When they cross the line coming in from practice, the line reminds them to be the best student they can be, the best person they can be.

Again, one of my concerns is that the influence of professionalism has been slowly creeping into the educational and athletic experiences of today's youth. Our goal at North Central College is to stay true to the pure core roots of our philosophy and to not be drawn into the ever-evolving pull of professionalism. Sport and running are not about outcome but rather about the person one becomes in the process.

Today's youth are not different from those I've coached over the years. However, it appears to me that the outside enticements and influences on them have changed. And unfortunately, the new leaders they're encouraged to follow seem to undermine the most important, unchanging personal standards of truth within themselves which lead to success in school, in a business, and certainly in sports.

I believe that the standards we should teach represent the nonnegotiable, eternal core truths that guide us throughout our lives. Absolute core concepts and ethics become a foundational "blueprint" for our rules for life as well as a support during adversity along the way. These behavioral ideals leading the athlete to personal bests are inseparable from the ideals for being the best you can be in life. The more virtuous the standards are, the more they'll help lead young people to better personal choices, and help them stand on a firmer personal foundation of strength.

To list the standards that guide me in this process in our cross country and track & field program at North Central College, I adhere to the following priority of guideposts. Our top guiding value is God, followed by family, academics, and (we hope) personal focus and commitment through the educational experience of athletics. We operate at North Central under the umbrella of Health and never compromise students' physical, mental, or spiritual health. Only after these priorities do we then rank our own track & field and cross country program decisions made within.

This order of values helps me in keeping the proper perspective when making decisions throughout our program. Several years ago, our All-American Brian Johnson, son of the Olympic sprints coach, Rob Johnson, came up to me one cold January afternoon and said, "Coach, I have a problem." I asked what it was. He stated that his sister was getting married. I said, "That is not a problem. That is a good thing!" He stated further that she was getting married in California. I replied that that was even better, since we were currently in the middle of winter here outside Chicago.

Then Brian said, "She is getting married in the spring on the same weekend as our conference championship." He asked what he should do. Without hesitation, I answered that he should go to his sister's wedding. After all, family is a priority over our athletic program. Now, to be honest, if he had told me he was going to skip the meet to take his girlfriend to the prom, I would have responded differently...

On another occasion, our freshman team was loading our van to compete at Knox College in the Small School State Collegiate Cross Country Championships, when I received a phone call from a college academic advisor concerning one of the freshmen on the traveling squad. The advisor indicated that this student had left a message on her desk asking her to drop him from a particular class and add him to any other class of her choice. I went back to our packed van and asked the freshman who had left the note to unpack his things. I told him he would not be making the trip and needed to go to his advisor's office to communicate why he was dropping the course and discuss with her the best course with which to replace it. He was not very happy with me, but academics takes priority over athletics.

Because of this value system, and our emphasis on academics as a priority over athletics, our cross country and track & field teams generally win recognition for the outstanding cumulative grade point average among athletic teams at North Central and throughout the nation. For the most part, our athletes have their own personal systems in the proper order. If they do not, then I will meet with them to help them realign and prioritize their values toward what we believe is most important about their athletic experience at North Central: education first, athletics second.

As John Denver wrote, "Some days are diamonds, and some days are stone." The North Central program is not about reaching those "diamond" days as an end goal. It's about how our student-athletes react, learn, and grow when they have both "diamond" days and "stone" days—and especially when the stone days outnumber the diamond. There is no "magic pond water" to help these athletes to deal with running's challenges, or life's. Our NCC program focuses on shepherding our athletes to do their best with the God-given ability they each have been blessed with, leading to stability, growth, and self-mastery. With the "qualified commitment" of an amateur, a student-athlete in mind, body, and spirit, our runners learn to cross that finish line as a whole, united person.

CHAPTER 4

Holistic Coaching—Laboratory for Life

"I am convinced that we understand 90% of the physiology in performance, but have only scratched the surface of understanding the magnitude of the influence of the unseen mysteries of the mind, heart, emotions, and spirit."

—Coach Al Carius

"Oddly enough, sometimes we want to help our children—and athletes—succeed so much that we end up bypassing experiences that stimulate important internal growth and development."

—Coach Al Carius

As I have stated, one of the advantages of teaching and coaching over 50 years in the same place is the opportunity to grow from my numerous mistakes and failures along the way. Oddly, I have been blessed with the chance to fail. As John Dewey noted, "Failure is instructive. The person who really thinks learns quite as much from his failures as from his successes." Michael Jordan was even more direct: "I've failed over and over again in my life. And that is why I succeed."

This sounds a bit absurd, doesn't it? However, recognizing when I have missed the mark as a coach has had emerging advantages for me when faced with similar situations throughout the years. Several such "failure is instructive" occasions came early in my coaching career. They helped me learn to appreciate a few of the many influences on an athlete's performance. Failure also helped me to grow and clarified my responsibility as a coach to make the best possible choices for the well-being of the athlete.

For beginners, there was the time during my first coaching year when I was asked by my good friend, Bill Leach, to speak at a clinic for Chicago inner-city coaches at the University of Illinois at Chicago. The topic was motivation. Judging from the lack of questions asked after my step-by-step textbook approach to the topic, the overwhelming response was... let's just say, I blew it. I did not understand the whole cultural background of the coaches I was addressing and the inner-city challenges they faced with relating to and motivating their athletes. My primary perspective was based on my isolated small-town experience and through my association with athletic teammates at Illinois.

Fortunately, following my uncomfortable presentation of motivational and physiological training methods, Ed Wallace, the coach from Steinmetz High School, spoke. Clearly, Wallace was a holistic, relational coach and understood his fellow coaches' inner-city world, its realities, and the people in it. Simply put, the heart of his message was that for some of his athletes, it was too often a difficult uphill struggle simply to feel worthy of success, when parts of their history were saturated with the feedback of negative experiences. His abundant insight hit the mark, while mine fell far short.

Ed emphasized the importance of first creating a positive atmosphere within his program, to help his athletes overcome the often-negative life challenges they encounter. Such a consistent, positive team setting then provided a more solid foundation for his athletes to achieve at the upper limit of their capabilities. Understanding the whole athlete and the influencing cultural environment surrounding him is critical, and Ed Wallace showed that a good coach's skills go beyond the simplistic thinking of physical training and external motivational techniques.

More to this point, another revelation of an early failure of mine, when our program was still young, was my decision to take a van of North Central athletes to a track meet at Indiana University. At the time, it was my opinion that, on the surface, our best North Central College athletes were physically capable of competing well at the Division I level and would benefit from the experience. Additionally, Indiana's program was down at the time, and the meet was being held for any athlete not making the traveling squad for one of the higher-level weekend meets like the Drake and Penn Relays. My evaluation was that there was not a depth of opposition talent remaining in the Indiana meet. I was confident we could be very competitive at this Division I meet with our select group of athletes.

Nonetheless, upon arrival at the meet site, one of our captains approached me and said, "Coach, we don't belong at this meet. We are just North Central College, and all of the schools are much bigger than we are." Being only one year removed from Big Ten competition myself, I felt my evaluation of our physical readiness for those chosen to compete at this level was correct. However, once again, I missed the mark as a coach by underestimating the whole unfamiliar situation for even my best athletes from a small college with a modest track program and a new coach.

On the whole, our athletes did not perform well that day. They were intimidated by the externals of the larger size and reputations of these Division I schools. Physically, we could compete, but mentally we were "psyched out" before the competition began. We were immobilized by a controlling emotion—fear. I had yet to learn the importance of program and team evolution, the athlete's deeper expectations and confidence, and my responsibility in influencing each. There would come a day for our Division III program when our athletes could run with, and even defeat, fine Division I programs. But we weren't there yet, neither mentally or spiritually, and my athletes knew it even if I didn't.

Finally, one last of many possible examples of superficial, simplistic thinking on my part from which I absorbed a very good lesson. In 1980, our freshman-dominated team had just won the Midwest NCAA Cross Country Regional hosted by Augustana College at the Credit Island course in Davenport, Iowa. We had approached the competition with no thoughts about outcome and certainly none of winning, just competing. Surprisingly we won the meet, with quiet minds focused on the process and our team, with great disbelief and excitement.

Mistakenly thinking I could give this young, inexperienced team a dose of "quick fix" mental confidence, I said upon reaching our van for the return home, "Now you know we can win nationals next week." After all, our senior-dominated teams had just won consecutive national championships in 1978 and 1979. I wanted the youngsters to feel they were at that level as well. The next week we dropped to seventh place in the NCAA Championships in Rochester, New York, while Augustana College and Luther College, the teams we had beaten the week before in Davenport, ended up taking second place and third place.

I was bewildered about how poorly we had performed after the spectacular finish just the week before. I asked each of the runners about their experience before, during, and after the competition. One by one, each expressed being nervous, with the first indicating he was so fearful the night before that he was shaking in his bed and another saying that he felt like he was going to throw up at the starting line.

I could not figure out what had changed during the week and called upon one of my Olympic mentors, Joe Newton of York High School in Elmhurst, for advice. I told him everything that transpired from regionals through the national meet. Immediately, he said it would have been much better, in hindsight, to have told the team in the van following regionals, "Great race! Now let's approach next week just as we did this week." He showed me how I had put pressure on this inexperienced group of young runners after their regional win, and created fear, by telling them they could now win nationals. Joe told me they felt more relaxed being the underdogs at regionals, but had not accumulated the genuine inner confidence to be the national favorites on center stage. We went from not thinking to over-thinking, from process-oriented to outcome-oriented individuals. Fear of failure is one of the greatest limiting factors in sports performance, and in life. We had yet to learn a lesson spoken of in the Bible 365 times—"Fear not." But how did I contribute to their fear?

Glenn Behnke, one of our first great All-Americans, was my assistant coach during the years of our early championships. He once said to me, "Coach, you always act differently the week of the conference championship." As a great athlete and coach himself, he could see in my early coaching behavior what I could not: my own tendency to sometimes focus on outcomes created pressure on our runners, and fear, instead of confidently allowing them to trust in our process to let the outcome "happen" as a result of our preparation. We find that fear is reduced on a team when "me" becomes "we." Since that time, I have consistently tried to be emotionally consistent throughout the entire season, treating each meet emotionally as I would the national championship.

Behnke, by the way, is another one of North Central's great "development" stories. A hardworking Milwaukee runner who never broke 60 seconds in the quarter-mile, Behnke at North Central ultimately ran a 4:12 mile, a sub-nine-minute two-mile, and 29:06.8 in the six-mile, a school record at the time. He placed third and second in the cross country nationals his junior and senior years. After winning the 1974 Division III six-mile at nationals as a senior, he placed 10th in the six-mile at the Division I national meet that year. His leadership and positive influence on our cross country program has been longstanding, and continues to this day.

To understand great performances, I have learned that one must go far beyond the consideration of the physical dimension. I am convinced that we understand ninety percent of the physiology in performance, but have only scratched the surface of understanding the magnitude of the influence of the unseen mysteries of the mind, heart, emotions, and spirit when blended together. I am not saying this from a qualified academic perspective, and please realize what I am not. No surprise, I am not a doctor, physiologist, nutritionist, psychologist, or minister. I am only a coach expressing my thoughts and perceptions formulated through years of trial, error, success, relationships, and insights from all. Let's just say that I should start everything I say with "It seems to me," rather than "This I know."

To get a glimpse of the nature of some of the underlying variables that contribute to the phenomenon of great performance, consider this study done at Harvard University. Instructors were each given a group of rats for an experiment on intelligence. The first instructor was told his rats were particularly bright and would learn very rapidly. During the same period, a second instructor was told his rats were of average intelligence and would progress at a normal rate. Finally, a third instructor was informed his rats were rather slow learners and would have genetic difficulty in completing the tasks to be mastered.

After the six-month controlled experiment was completed, the test results showed that the rats in each group performed at the level of expectation presented to their instructor. What the instructors didn't know was that the potential to learn for each group of rats was the same. In fact, they all came from the same litter and were therefore of equal ability. It turned out that the main finding for the difference in performance of the three groups of rats was explained by the level of expectation exhibited by each instructor. The instructors, it seems, expected more or less of their rats based on how the intelligence of their rats had been framed for them. And their enhanced or diminished expectations for their charges showed up in the subsequent performances of each group of rats. Keep in mind that, even with no direct spoken communication, the influence of tone and body language of each instructor may have affected the performance of their charges.

That's it. Time out. Hey, I know this study involved rats, so what does this have to do with running and performance? Good question. More to that point, the same experiment was undertaken with students as subjects. No surprise here: after one year, the results remained the same. The subjects of the second study, students, performed only up to the level expected of them by their instructors. Why is this? The answer is simple: as coaches and teachers, we often get from others exactly what we expect to get.

Clearly, our words and actions communicate many different messages such as confidence and expectations. For the proper effects to take place, the teaching or coaching process takes day-by-day consistency, patience, and our encouraging reinforcement. What the findings of the Harvard study suggest is that the way we communicate to ourselves and to others accumulates within the subconscious mind, leaving a powerful impact on our self-image and self-confidence in performance. Many factors beyond the science of training the body can supersize a performance to its highest level. This alone might not qualify us to do anything, but it does allow us to do everything we do *better*. Bruce Lee was quoted as saying, "As we think, so shall you become."

Once again, I return to my conversation with my good friend Jim Braun, the Waubonsie Valley High School counselor. As is often the case, I enjoy learning from people with expertise beyond mine. Admittedly, those exchanges are numerous. Jim, as you recall, had indicated to me that many students today either don't know the steps necessary to reach their goals or lack the wisdom and work ethic needed to bridge the gap between where they are and where they want to go.

His feedback also started me thinking about my own scholastic training background. I recalled the questionnaire I once received after graduating from Morton High School asking me to evaluate my educational experience there and the effect it had had on my life since graduation. Certainly, I was taught many tools in the classroom, but there is so much more to education than facts, figures, grades, and report cards. Much of my understanding of the successful pursuit of goals was learned outside the classroom and was absorbed within my mind, body, and spirit—often in the gymnasium and on the athletic fields.

More specifically, running itself became a living mode for me to gain a greater exposure to the wisdom of self-discovery. Through running, I uncovered many benefits and patterns of behavior important to raising levels of achievement—not just for me, but for the athletes I would coach: for example, commitment, discipline, motivation, focus, work ethic, loyalty, teamwork, dealing with adversity, dealing with success, and positive expectations.

Many of these "internal characteristics of success" were modeled for me when I got to know Dick Butkus in the spring of 1961 at the University of Illinois. He was a good friend of Bob Easter who I had known from Richwoods High School in Peoria. Needless to say, Butkus was a big name on campus as well as throughout the collegiate football scene. Dick and I were both in the same physical education course at the University of Illinois. One segment of the PE course consisted of our participation in a series of physical fitness activities. My first thought was that Dick would scheme a case for being exempt from those tests. After all, he was Dick Butkus. *Why would he have to prove his fitness?*

However, he enthusiastically and aggressively competed through every test. He was first in the rope climb, first in the agility run, and first in all of the activities leading up to the three-mile run. That run started from Huff Gymnasium, went around the agronomy farms, and finished back at the gymnasium. I finally felt at home in one of these physical tests. In my mind, I thought for sure Dick would be excused or excuse himself from a cardiovascular run or short of that, at the very least, he would run it as easy as possible. Words just don't do a justice in explaining how much respect he earned from me that very warm spring day as he huffed and puffed his way, competing to the best of his ability, from start to finish in that three-mile run.

Though physically he was gifted, something more profound caught my attention about the Dick Butkus who would go on to become one of professional football's finest performers for the Chicago Bears. It was beyond his mindset, and within his internal radar—his competitive spirit. The main point of all this: coming in first did not matter to him but challenging himself to be his best in the process did. He expected to do well and give his best. And he once expressed it this way, "When you step into the arena, you can let it overwhelm you or let it take you to a higher level." Dick never let it overwhelm him.

Then, there is the story of one of my former runners at North Central College, Dan Baker, from Rushville, Illinois. By comparing times, records, and accomplishments, Baker was one of the most successful middle-distance runners in the history of our school. But again, my point is not about his external accomplishments but rather what influenced the process guiding him to reach that level of success. Dan had run a 1:58 in the 800 meters at Rushville. But, his high school coach, Dick Tucker, recommended Dan to us because of his attitude, telling me, "Dan Baker is a quality human being."

There was never a question in my mind of the source of his focused spirit. "I would say I came in as a nobody," Baker recalled in an interview on our NCC website. "I excelled because of two things—being brought up with a very diligent work ethic and having Al Carius and the coaching staff there."

"I had trained little during high school, and when it came time to go to college, the first practice was terrible," Baker said. "I started joining the distance runners for morning runs after Christmas break my sophomore year, and it made all the difference." It became evident throughout his four years of running that Dan's training evolved, and his performances improved after that Christmas break, as he adopted our common core patterns of behavior. There was never a question that his servo-mechanism was on autopilot, guiding him to each new goal he would set for himself. Dan became a 2-time Division III national champion, in the 1500 meters and the 800 meters. He posted his personal best times of 3:51.09 in the 1500 meters and 1:49.9 in the 800 meters, while becoming a 7-time All-American.

After his graduation, I received a phone call from a personnel director at a Chicago corporation asking for an unbiased recommendation for Baker. It seemed the job had come down to a choice between Baker and another candidate. I assured the caller that within a short period of time Dan's work-ethic and character would reveal him to be the right choice. Baker was hired and one year later took a personal day off from work to come back to North Central College to visit the team, the coaching staff, and me.

While Dan was gone that day, rumors began to circulate throughout his office that Baker could be interviewing for another job in his absence. When he returned to work the next day after visiting us at NCC, he was promptly called into his supervisor's office and given a raise in pay. See what a personal day can do?! I will never forget Dan calling me and laughing about the experience.

There probably is not a week that goes by when I am not giving one of my former athletes a similar recommendation for some position. In each case, there are never questions about track & field or cross country performances, but rather the questions always deal with the character of the individual. Dan himself was very soft spoken, but never had to speak much because, as Emerson said, complimenting, "What you *are* shouts at me so loudly I can hardly hear what you are saying."

I am always recharged with each call, text, email, or visit from those who have helped our program evolve to its present level—our alumni and friends. One of the great joys of teaching and coaching, in addition to helping support athletes progress and reach their stated competitve goals, is the ongoing relationships I have with my athletes beyond the four-year collegiate experience. I am elated every time one of my former student-athletes takes the time to stay connected with me. I savor every one of those contacts. But the greatest satisfaction I have is seeing the maturation of our athletes after they leave our program, learning and knowing that somehow they took something valuable away with them from their experience in track & field and cross country.

Every now and again I hear from or see my former runner Tony Rizzo. Tony and I are forever intertwined through the coach-athlete relationship we shared during his four years at North Central College. It is a great gift I will treasure. Clearly, he continues to grow each time I see or hear from him. What struck me the last time I saw him was that he was much more disciplined and self-assured than he had been even as the outstanding runner who had earned twelve NCAA All-American awards while at North Central College.

During his running years, Tony's performances—along with those of his teammate Ryan Board—often reflected a concept first explained by Oregon coach Bill Bowerman. What Bowerman suggested was that no matter how thorough the plan, or how well-trained and prepared an athlete on a team is for competition, one critical factor must be internally in place for a truly successful performance—a flexible, adaptable response system for the unexpected situations which spontaneously occur during athletic competition. The coach dress rehearses and prepares the athlete and team for every possible scenario in competition. But, inevitably, the unanticipated will appear and how you respond *in that moment* will have an effect on the outcome. That response is what Bowerman labeled "competitive response."

Tony was a master during these reflexive-now moments. He did not want to overthink or put mental clutter into his mind before any competition. Often, he would tell me before meets, "Don't say anything about how to run the race. Just let me react as the race develops." Interestingly, this attitude was similar to that of the great Australian distance runner, Herb Elliot, who indicated that he had no pre-race strategy, only to compete and run his race. Although he was small in size, Tony was a competitive giant in heart. He was never fearful or intimidated by anything or anyone.

His "competitive response" was brilliant on the track but occasionally became impulsive off the track, clouding some of his personal decisions. We shared those moments, the good and the challenging, both growing from them.

I often referred to Tony as my Billy Martin, the scrappy, confident second baseman and later manager for the New York Yankees. Whatever Billy Martin was a part of in Yankee baseball as a player and manager, they won. Tony ran with Martin's winning focus, an intense aggressiveness that intimidated opposing runners, and supersized his teammates' performances with his passion and air of confidence. He did not like to lose. Just as Martin knew and felt the pride of the Yankee pinstripes, Tony valued the rich tradition of the North Central College candy striped uniform. (More on this in Chapter 8.) He felt and owned the feeling of our tradition deep within himself.

Although he knew how to prepare and focus himself for racing, Tony's first loyalty was always to his teammates. On one occasion in 1998, we were headed into a very significant cross country meet, and our team was weakened with illness. At the time, Tony himself was sidelined with an injury and his readiness for competition was questionable. By competing in this meet, he would forfeit the opportunity to hardship the season, which would have allowed him to repeat the current season the next year when he was better prepared and healthy. In addition, competing at that time could have aggravated his condition. Upon learning of our team's vulnerability, he immediately showed up at my office door insisting upon his readiness and intention to run in the meet—really no surprise there, knowing his competitiveness. He ran despite his injury, and Tony's presence on that day synergized our collective team confidence with his loyalty and 78th place finish. "Loyalty," Mario Puzo wrote, "is the strongest glue, which makes a relationship last for a lifetime." Tony, like so many of our athletes, learned, exhibited, and benefited from loyalty as a member of a team.

Every time I hear from Tony I have more and more respect from him. You see, he joined the Marines, became a great leader and coach, and now is a proud father and husband. I am so very proud of his personal growth and his lasting legacy of great "competitive response" in the pressure of competition.

These are but a few examples where athletics revealed and contributed to the personality development of our athletes through their experience within the process. Athletics can help place the participants in the best environment for exposure to learn the attributes of success that help lead them to their goals. Readiness and positioning are two keys to helping athletes change and unlock the answers to their "why." The most appropriate athletic positioning can assist the student-athlete to grow and to change from the inside out. This, of course, is a difficult process if the student-athlete has not answered the "why" question in his life.

Oddly enough, change is very often the topic of conversation in our coaches' offices at North Central College. During these discussions, the question is often raised, "Do people really change?" It really is a tough question. Keep in mind that not everything we teach in a classroom or in athletics has the desired results that we hope for, and again as a teacher-coach, I do not believe I can motivate or change anyone. I can only reinforce the spark or fire which they have found deep within themselves which leads them to their goal. In my opinion, the spark necessary for authentic change, to move a person from one place to another, comes through faith in a higher power. Some call it a "defining moment," a "decisive moment," "crunch time," or "a wake-up call." Coaches are often in a position to help the student-athlete make a change for the better when the time is right and the individual is ready. John Wooden noted that "a coach is someone who can give correction without causing resentment."

Have you ever had a wakeup call in your life? The light goes on and you have the "ah hah" moment, the "moment of truth" that provides the real catalyst to change your life. Personally, I have been there a few times—that feeling cutting into the depth of your being, igniting a fire, cleaning your head of life's clutter, and forever allowing you to feel and see your core blueprint. Keep in mind, this is not to suggest these calls are much fun, but rather they are a crossroads offering you a choice for a second chance, through change to the core of your soul.

It turns out this wakeup call is vividly illustrated in one of my favorite movies, *Groundhog Day*. Right off the bat, my first impression was the movie would be pretty dull and boring. Think about it: The storyline has Bill Murray reliving the same day over and over again. Murray's selfish character thought his experience was dull and boring too, as the repetition led him through stages of his selfishness: fear, boredom, emptiness, pain, and finally to his life's crossroads.

At this point, he discovered his inner-self and the courage to stop trying to control others during his day. He taught himself to focus on changing himself rather than trying to control and change others. He maximized life's growth-producing process through his repetition of a single day, a journey of self-discovery leading to the steps of selflessness, service to others, and self-mastery. He rediscovered what is most important and what is not. This may be a surprise to some, but I found this Bill Murray movie to be very religious because of the spiritual life lessons he learned each day as the movie progressed.

Motivation and spirit are very personal and based upon each person's depth of thinking and intentions to accomplish a goal. As a coach, I can only reinforce what an athlete chooses to do. The law of readiness states that when a person is ready to learn, the teacher will come serendipitously into their life. Like it or not, the simple truth is that, as a teacher, I cannot make everyone learn, nor as a coach can I make someone run. Clearly, the imperative spark must be present within the individual first. They must reach their "defining moment," be ready to learn, and have found their "why."

Here is a concrete example. For two years, I had done my best to motivate a particular student-athlete, Julius White, both in the classroom and on the track, to perform up to his God-given talent and potential. He was a very intelligent young man and a very gifted runner. Unfortunately, he had learned how to just get by with his natural gifts, making him a marginal student and an average athlete. During this time, his words were consistently reassuring me of his satisfactory academic progress, but many of the telltale signs indicated a profound disconnection between his words and grades. It was also very apparent to me that he was underperforming as an athlete. His crossroads moment came when he was dismissed from school because of his lack of progress in the classroom.

What happened? Predictably, he came to inform me of his disappointment at being dismissed. Mistakenly, I thought he had reached the deepest level of his soul for this initial crossroads moment, and would change. After helping him write a letter of appeal, he was reinstated into the college only to return to his pattern of just getting by. Once again, he was dismissed from the college and again came to me for assistance. This time I refused, telling him I could not contribute to his digging himself deeper into his hole academically and financially. He left North Central College and attended a community college for a time.

To his great credit, Julius was not bitter about being dismissed twice from North Central. After a semester or two, he once again came to my office saying he wanted to return to run for North Central. At this point, there was something different about him—his look, the feeling with which he spoke, and his words were now connected to a much deeper influence: his spirit. Sometimes the pain thrust upon us at life's crossroads provides lessons and opportunities that stimulate real changes in attitude and behavior.

To this day, I state to everyone that Julius is one of the most intelligent, intuitive young men I have ever known. He matured through his opportunities to change and grow through his choices. He turned his mistakes into opportunities for him to graduate, to become a multi-All-American athlete, and a highly successful lifetime friend. My mistake was not becoming a better holistic coach in his life sooner. He graduated and has a family of his own whom I often get the good fortune to have as a part of my life.

These are choices we make daily in life's cafeteria line, and are ever-present choices as we decide over time what we will absorb from each experience and every person we meet. Whenever I drive from Naperville to my hometown of Morton, I always have a choice of which route I will take—to get home faster on the fast-lane highways of Interstates 55 and 74, or to slow down and return on the two-lane routes of 24 and 116. Most times, I ponder and choose the routes that most helped shape me into who I am today—two-lane State Highways through El Paso (Sunday smorgasbord dinners with my family at the Elms), Gridley (night track meets with friends like Ducky Baum), Eureka (basketball games with Dawdy, Paluska, Kelch, and Johnson), Goodfield (Mom and Dad's favorite restaurant, called Busy Corner), Deer Creek (night softball for fun with my friends), my brother Jim coaching at Deer Creek Grade School, relatives, and Kennel Lake (the checkpoint on my six-mile loop south of Morton that overlooked its lights on many an evening run).

Things haven't changed much along the slower route home, but the life lessons I learned and the memories I cherish are always worth the extra time. I recall especially *what I learned about myself* on Kennel Lake runs, viewing the distant glowing lights of Morton. Call it visualization or call it practice. The pictures I created in my mind during these runs became my reality for countless future races, and helped me develop my own "competitive response" to the conditions and numerous levels of future competition. In short, I created the outcome of future races by what I thought and became on these training runs. I became on these runs what I wanted to become: a runner. I didn't realize it at the time, but I was confirming Emerson again. He noted that, "A great part of courage is the courage of having done the thing before."

The fact is, no one even witnessed any of these imagined races because I had created every situation and condition in my mind. Nobody else knew I was there—alone in the dark quiet of a country road. Regardless, when the mental pictures were authentic enough, the body responded physically and emotionally to my imagination with a synergy of mind, body, heart, and spirit. That synergy energized my experience, and allowed for a transfer of positive "expectations of confidence" for subsequent performances—specificity from visualization.

Certainly, the thoughts in our mind, with the influence of our spirit, have a potent effect on actual or perceived reality in our lives. Remember, William James noted that "Man can alter his life by altering his thinking." Consequently, whatever we want to become, we need to create first in our mind with a personal goal, and then nurture and reinforce with what we see, with what we hear, what (and whom) we surround ourselves with, and what we say to ourselves. It is our daily choice. Think like, act like, train like the runner—or the person—you want to become. The responsibility of being a holistic coach includes sharing these insights with ones athletes. But more, it involves shaping a similar successful process for the involvement of the body, mind, and spirit of the athletes one is privileged to coach.

CHAPTER 5

Three Levels of Coaching: The Body (Level 1–Physiology of Exercise, 1960s)

"Ideally, sport is not about being the best but rather about doing the best that you can within the boundaries and realities of your life."

—Coach Al Carius

"Dr. Jeff Duke's holistic 'Three Levels of Coaching' objectified my intuition."

—Coach Al Carius

"Treat your body like a temple, not a woodshed. The mind and body work together. Your body needs to be a good support system for the mind and spirit. If you take good care of it, your body can take you wherever you want to go, with the power and strength and energy and vitality you will need to get there."

—Jim Rohn

n 2009, while attending the USTFCCCA National Coaches Convention in Orlando, I had the enlightening opportunity to hear Dr. Jeff Duke speak on the topic, "Motivating the 21st

Century Athlete." Dr. Duke is a Christian sports psychologist. I was mesmerized by his message. He classified coaches into three levels, based on the complexity and style of their coaching. Although I will not get hung up on his exact percentages because I believe they are ever-changing, his concept of the three levels of coaching was very meaningful to me.

He indicated at that time that he believed 80% of coaches focus primarily on skills and training the athlete's body, and fall into the Level 1, "Science and Technique" group of coaching. Next, he indicated that 15% of coaches have evolved to Level 2, and blend a focus on the mind in dualism with the physical training of the body. Finally, he communicated that only 5% of coaches combine holistically the mind, body, and spirit (passion) within their coaching philosophy and approach, Level 3. Dr. Duke also noted that whenever you find a program that has a consistency of success, you will find a Level 3 coach.

I found Dr. Duke's concept of the three different levels of coaching very insightful and reinforcing to what I already intuitively felt inside about coaching at your best. His lecture and also his book, *3 Dimensional Coaching*, helped me to frame his three levels of coaching within this book. I believe some of the very best coaches have reached Dr. Duke's Third Level of coaching—John Wooden at UCLA, Ted Haydon at Chicago, Tony Dungy, Mike Krzyzewski at Duke, Phil Jackson, Gary Wilson, Dean Smith, Bill Walsh, and Ed Wallace to name just a few examples. The concepts of these categories can also be applied to athletes and, for that matter, almost anyone in my opinion. Ed Mathey, our baseball coach, once said this to me: "Coaches who know how, coach. The ones who don't, measure."

Certainly, my educational coaching training at the University of Illinois in the 1960's was all Level 1 education based purely upon coaching of "the physical." Anatomy, physiology, physiology of exercise, kinesiology, fitness classes, first aid, and technique for wrestling, football, basketball, gymnastics, baseball, and track and field—everything in my coaching training was focused on the science of conditioning, training, and learning skills in each of the various sports. At that time, one of the leading experts on human performance at the University of Illinois, Dr. Thomas K. Cureton, explained nearly every breakthrough in sport, such as Roger Bannister's first sub-four-minute mile, with physiological data such as stroke volume of the heart, red blood cell count, capillaries, VO^2 max, coefficient of oxygen utilization, and vital capacity.

Whenever I am asked to speak, most coaches ask, "What are your workouts?" Fewer coaches want to hear me talk about the more meaningful, intangible contributing factors of mind and spirit which help raise the physical to higher levels of performance. Basically, there are no real secrets within our workouts or our physical instruction training at North Central, as you will see. Once the athlete grasps the concepts and principles of a system, the specificities fall into place and provide individuals many options. Principles and concepts are the program's absolutes and truths that serve as the foundation for the standards and details of the training structure. The athlete gains great confidence through understanding the framework, and improves by implementing the best personal choices to meet the objective of the concept or principle. Our basic physiological conception is: "Aerobic strength creates speed beyond 40 meters."

Simply put, the improvement of one's endurance as a runner depends on the cardiovascular and respiratory systems, efficiency in transporting oxygen and nutrients to the tissues, and the body's ability to rid itself of the waste products (carbon dioxide, lactic acid, etc.) produced in the process. Essentially, increasing the body's efficiency to take in and utilize oxygen is the key to improving endurance performance or one's aerobic range of speed. We are born with a genetic basic level of speed which is sometimes measured with our best 40-meter sprint time. Speed is innate to 40 meters, while endurance is enhanced by building the efficiency of the cardio-respiratory systems to aerobically allow us to maintain speed beyond 40 meters to the selected distance we are choosing to race.

Once again, this was objectified for me at a U.S. Track & Field and Cross Country Coaches clinic. I was fortunate to hear a presentation, by nine-time Olympic Gold Medalist Carl Lewis, reinforcing this physiology. At that time, Carl said something that I believe is the basis of all endurance performances. He indicated that a sprinter reaches his maximum speed at about 40 meters. He went on to state that he beat many of his opponents because they began to decelerate past 40 meters and he was able to maintain his speed through 100 meters. This being true, it means that our own ability to control and to maintain our momentum determines our ultimate time over all distances past 40 meters. We do not get faster than our natural speed, but we get aerobically stronger to build endurance "glue" to sustain our pace through the varying distances of a race.

Improbable as it may seem, in my opinion, many non-athletes could cover the distance of a marathon—especially if it were a strong personal goal—as long as the energy source was available, and the person went conservatively enough. Let's be clear, this is not to suggest that anyone can go out and try a marathon without medical clearance and proper long-term preparation. Ultimately, the distance is not as big a factor in the successful completion of a run as is the body's ability efficiently to supply the oxygen and nutrients, and rid itself of the waste products, as the speed of the effort increases from standing to walking to running. Sustaining a pace is the challenge and one's ability to do so can be enhanced through the proper aerobic training. Again, "aerobic strength determines speed beyond 40 meters."

The physiology is well-known and documented. Nearly everyone can take advantage of the benefits of running and see his or her times improve through positive adaptation of their training. But one's training must be done with the specificity of tempo, consistency, and patience to allow it to work in a progressive overload process. The athlete's aerobic range will improve through increased red blood cells (which carry oxygen), increased capillaries (the pipeline of the blood exchange to tissues), increased stroke volume of the heart (the amount of blood pumped from the left ventricle per beat of the heart), and also with numerous other adjustments made with progressively administered specific cardiovascular exercises. Some terminology used to describe these processes includes "coefficient of oxygen utilization," "oxygen uptake," and "oxygen utilization."

The tricky part is that there are too many individual variables (age, body type, weight, present condition, diet, weather, and numerous other individual variables) for me to confidently recommend specific training schedules within the confines of a book. I would refer readers primarily interested in more detailed scientific physiology or training to read Joe Vigil's book *Road to the Top* and Jack Daniels's book *Running Formula*, or the many other excellent options for distance training.

Our training system at North Central College is very simple and adheres to the scientific, time-proven physiology of exercise for the cardiovascular system. But I did not always understand these basic principles and had to go through an evolutionary process of trial and error to clarify the proper physiology to implement for North Central College. Very basically, our training of the body at North Central is related directly to one of our mottos: "Aerobic strength determines anaerobic potential." Or, put another way, "Aerobic strength is speed." Our plan of training distance runners is based on the same concept, with the specifics varying with the individual athlete's background, physiology, maturity, and targeted goal distance. Together, we build a strong aerobic base as the glue that holds an athlete's genetic speed together for his race distance past 40 meters, as per the enlightening information from Carl Lewis.

To help explain this need for, and the importance of, a strong aerobic foundation in distance running, here is some interesting data. Robert Chapman, PhD, Adjunct Professor of Kinesiology at Indiana University, presented this information while speaking at a clinic I attended. It summarizes the percentages for the aerobic and the anaerobic contribution to races from 400 meters to the marathon:

Anaerobic v Aerobic Effort in Races	Anaerobic %	Aerobic %
Marathon	1	99
10k	3	97
5k	6	94
3k	12	88
1500m	23	77
800m	40	60
400m	57	43

Though God-given genetic speed is an advantage from point "0" (the start) to 40 meters, it is the runner's ability to take in oxygen and distribute it along with nutrients to the active tissue cells—and then remove the waste products as efficiently as possible—that determines the athlete's level of endurance, or ability to sustain this speed. You cannot fake aerobic strength. But, endurance can be built through understanding the body's ability to adapt to specific progressive overload, and patiently and consistently implementing flexibility within training to fit the reality of individual needs.

Our plan of training for a typical week, outlined below, is as follows. We have two training sessions per day, Monday through Friday, starting with a short, easy run at 6:30 a.m. This run acts as a way to open up the cardiovascular system and clean out the waste products from the day before. It also allows us to start the day with positive self-discipline and a "win" for the rest of the day. The athlete will feel better, physically and mentally, in the afternoon because of this gentle morning session.

These morning runs are also great team-builders, as banter, storytelling, and individual athlete's quirky personalities flourish in the easy-going atmosphere. Any morning run might randomly feature a "Mr. Temperature" quiz, "Joe's Jokes," "Name that Desert," or other creative banter. We also benefited over the years by the presence in our morning packs of wise and funny older runners and NCC alumni from our Naperville community. "Big Daddy" Bob Schrader used to ask us History quiz questions prepared for his junior high classes. Sheldon "Moose" Hayer, Paul Rewerts, Hal Carlson, Chuck Carroll, Eric Thornton, and Dick Ruzicka are just a few of the many local gems who delighted our runners over the years. They helped put the "fun" in our Run for Fun program.

Monday: Building tempo run, 10-12 miles. Or, Variation running (intervals or fartlek)

In my opinion, "building tempo" runs are a major key to successful distance running. I have seen this benefit reinforced numerous times with eight- to twelve-mile building tempo runs. Craig Virgin, Ron Clarke, and Gerry Lindgren are known to have celebrated the positive effects of building tempo runs on their world-class performances. The great Illinois and US runner and world champion, Craig Virgin, once told me that his "performances took off" after he began running negative splits on his training runs.

The Australian legend, Ron Clarke, addressed tempo runs in a wonderful 1995 article, "*The myth of long slow running.*" Clarke noted, "We covered 16 to 20 kilometers each evening most, if not every week day, 50 or so weeks in the years. But it wasn't slow. We used to get faster and faster as the session progressed… It was no disgrace to drop out—sometimes one or the other would have a great night and would run clear away early on, but the general pattern was to settle into a rhythm, *then gradually increase the tempo.*" [emphasis added]

It's hard to find a better recommendation for "building tempo" runs than this one from the man who broke 17 official world track records at various long distances in the 1960s. Clarke believed there were initial short-term benefits to interval training. But, he noted that there are no breaks in the middle of a race, and tempo runs do a better job of simulating the reality of a race.

I have to remind my readers here that great as Clarke was, my personal angel and teammate from Kansas, Billy Mills, *beat* Ron Clarke (and Muhammed Gammoudi) down the straightaway to win the 10,000 meter final in 1964 at the Tokyo Olympics. Amazingly, Billy ran *two* personal best performances that day in one race, passing 5,000 meters in a PR on the way to winning at 10,000 meters in a PR and an Olympic record time. His Wikipedia entry records another important goal for runners: "Mills has stated that he tried to be relaxed during his final kick to the finish line and felt that helped him pass both Gammoudi and Clarke." I will have more to say later about this goal of "relaxing and being in the moment" while racing. Admittedly, Clarke did beat Mills when both ran the marathon later in those Olympic games in Tokyo, but I just had to remind you what a great athlete my friend Billy Mills was.

Here at North Central College, many of our greatest runners relied on these "run faster as you go farther" runs: Dan Mayer, Jeff Milliman, John Weigel, Dru Patel, Colin Young, Tim McCoskey, Glenn Behnke, Johnny Crain, Tony Bleull, Matt Brill, Derron Bishop, Jim Dickerson, Brian Henz, Rich Scopp, Bob Dunphey, Rich Scott, and Jeff Stiles to name a few. These North Central runners produced dozens of All-American honors among them.

If we choose Interval training for Monday, our pattern is this: a 5-mile building tempo run to a grass park, where we do 4 short-rest (90 seconds jog between) mile repeats at upper-level aerobic pace. We stress negative splitting for the progression of each mile. This is followed by 6 strides and a 1-mile cool down. A substitute for these repeat miles might be fartlek runs. This Monday workout comes closest to the specificity of a competitive race, since we emphasize the four parts of a race throughout the four repeat miles. And we start each mile at a specific time to match the tension of the start of the race.

Tuesday: Recovery Day. Easy aerobic run, 1 hour

Tuesday is our day to recover physically, mentally, and emotionally. I believe emotional stress is the biggest cause of fatigue there is. Years ago, the University of Oregon did a study to see how many days in a row they could train their distance runners hard before they would break down. Only Bill Dellinger lasted 7 days before breaking down, physically. All the other athletes tested faltered along the way. "No-stress Tuesday is designed for us to recover mentally, physically, and emotionally. We call Tuesday "the night of our Day."

Wednesday: Hill Day. 5-mile tempo run + 6 times hills/100 yards + 3 miles fartlek home

There is great magic and benefit to running hills. I have always felt this to be true even before I learned the physiological science behind it. They provide positive anaerobic effects without speed—slower and faster runners obtain similar anaerobic benefits—and help produce mental toughness as well. I tell our runners before our first hill workout of the year, "This hill will never change, but you will change each week as you get stronger." Their hill work becomes a great gauge for their growth from week to week and season to season. We concentrate on getting to the top with our focus on one step at a time.

Hill repeats are certainly an important part of our North Central workouts, but their benefits are probably obvious to most runners and coaches. I'd like to focus on our occasional fartlek workouts, which I consider to be the *best* form of interval training or variation running for our runners. Once an athlete understands the principles of fartlek training, it opens up multiple options for an individual to fit the workout to their personal training goals, fitness level, and sense of their own health on the day of the workout. We do encourage runners to be at the upper level of their comfort zone during the pickups to simulate a tempo run, with a short (jogging) rest in between to simulate a tempo run.

But no coach can know the appropriate number or intensity of the pickups a runner should include on any given day.

With fartlek training, the athlete himself (or herself) controls intuitively the four variables of the workout—the distance covered, the intensity of their effort, the rest period between intervals, and the number of repetitions. A valuable bonus, for the runner and the coach, is that the athlete will gain confidence from designing his own effective workout. They come to believe in the workout and take ownership of it, because they built it themselves. And the athlete can continually use that experience as a reference feeling for their future workouts and racing.

Thursday: Aerobic tempo run up to 70 minutes

Thursday is not a repeat of Tuesday's run. But it does have the advantage of recovery while on an aerobic distance run longer than Tuesday's.

Friday: Building tempo run up to 5 miles and 3 miles of fartlek, or Race

Once again, I believe tempo runs provide the greatest specificity for preparation to race and are the best preparation for racing *other than the race itself.* Ron Clarke, who promoted tempo runs as beneficial, also believed that racing specificity could be used as an important part of distance training. Racing over and under your preferred racing distance provides specific benefits to aerobic and anaerobic development, as well as confidence from the experience. For example, a 1500 meter runner should benefit from running an 800 meter for anaerobic speed and benefit as well while running the 5,000 meters for aerobic strength. Racing can be an integral part of training when not concerning yourself with the outcome. What better racing specificity can you get than actually racing?

Saturday: Long run up to 2 hours

The advantage of the long run for distance runners is well accepted. But achieving appropriate longer distances over time must be built up to through "progressive overload," and patience. One wouldn't send a new or a very young runner on extended distance runs. To make a comparison to weightlifting, a coach wouldn't ask an athlete to lift 100 pounds until it was clear the athlete could safely lift, for example, 20 and 40 and 60 pounds first. The same progressive overload concept applies to distance running.

Three-time Olympian Jim Spivey emphasized the physiological importance for successful distance runners of long runs similar to ours. He cited Dr. David Martin, one of the world's leading research physiologists on distance runners. Dr. Martin's research suggested that great physiological changes benefiting the body occurred during runs of 45 minutes and beyond. A corollary was that one 60-minute run produced more physiological benefits than two 30-minute runs.

Sunday: Easy aerobic run, 30 minutes to 1 hour, or Rest

Sunday is a day of rest and recovery and church. The athlete's intuition is the best guide to meeting this purpose. What's appropriate? Anything from nothing to a short run to open up and clean out the cardiovascular system, and clear the mind.

This foundation of weekly aerobic mileage may and will vary throughout the year. But it is important to maintain since its benefits will start to diminish after about four weeks. It takes a long time to develop this strong aerobic base, but it can be lost quickly if neglected after this four-week period. The mileage per week will vary with each athlete but will range between 50 and 100 miles per week. Remember, "The shoe that fits one person pinches another; there is no recipe for living [or running] that suits all cases." Carl Jung

As stated, Level 1 training, with the objective science in the education of the physical, is understood by 80% of our coaches. I venture to say that nearly 100% of our coaches have a pretty good grasp of the effects of training on the body because they can be tested and seen. The more difficult levels for coaches and their athletes are Levels 2 and 3, which involve training athletes *through* the physical with a focus on the invisible influence of the mind and spirit. I will discuss my approach to and thoughts about these levels in the following chapters.

Levels 2 and 3 of coaching are really not an exact science like exercise science, and as a result, the evidence is not as clear. These levels are more intangible and deal more with faith in the unseen, correlations and, above all, holistic connected relationships. Their influences are ultimately felt with "gut" insight—you know when the process is there and you know when it is not. It is an art, almost a gift, and it involves emotions and feelings more than the measurable physical. Intuition is a collective, internal "sixth sense" that binds the mind, body, and spirit together in a holistic way. Johanne Kaspar Lavater called intuition "The clear conception of the whole at once."

———————

Have you ever felt something was missing deep within you that helps define who you are? Well, as I have already stated, I felt that way during my first semester at the University of Kansas in the fall of 1960. For some reason I didn't understand at the time, running just didn't feel the same anymore. The physical was there but my mind, heart, and soul were not. At this point, I transferred to the University of Illinois in hopes of finding what I had lost and what was missing from the joy I had experienced in high school athletics. I thought at Illinois I would find the perfect quick-fix physical training plan and that would be my answer to the void I was feeling deep within me.

Ironically, Leo Johnson, the head track coach at Illinois in January of 1961, was also looking for answers. During the same period, Johnson had developed the Illinois system for training distance runners, and it was built around the training of University of Illinois runner George Kerr, who had been the bronze medalist in the 1960 Olympic 800 meters at Rome. Kerr was a Jamaican athlete who studied at the U of I, and continued to train with us while in graduate school. Back then, the Illinois distance team met in the basement classroom of Huff Gymnasium each Monday to review the weekly training plan based on whatever Kerr was doing. The pattern was predictable with little variation through most of the winter indoor season.

During this time, Kerr traveled to the West Coast to compete against an athlete coached by the great Hungarian national team coach, Mihaly Igloi. Igloi was known for training his athletes in spikes on the track nearly every day as well as for his nearly exclusive use of interval training, basically glorified wind sprints. Igloi used varying sets of different distances to train his athletes, rarely exceeding 400 meters for each repetition. The number of repetitions in each set, the speed, and the distances of the repetitions were randomly called out to the athletes during the workouts. The volume of repetitions and sets were extremely high compared with the numbers recommended by most American coaches who were using interval training at the time. Igloi basically created the workout variables intuitively throughout each training session, with no predetermined pattern to begin the workout.

Unfortunately, George Kerr lost the race to Igloi's athlete. The following Monday, Coach Johnson called us to our weekly meeting and informed us of a radically different training schedule from that which we had grown accustomed; it included a high volume of repetitions of intervals done on the track in spikes. Our previous model of intervals had involved very few intervals at high-level speed with longer rests in between each repetition.

Several weeks later, Kerr competed in another indoor meet and lost again. This time the loss came to an athlete coached by Arthur Lydiard, the New Zealand national team coach. Lydiard's emphasis in training was on high weekly mileage done on the roads in training flats. You guessed it. The next week, we were back in the meeting room in the basement of Huff Gymnasium on Monday and back at the chalkboard with Johnson, who explained our newest system of training which emphasized up to 100 miles per week on the roads. Coach Johnson laid out our daily workouts with the target of 100 miles by the following Sunday. Soon after this meeting, to no one's surprise, my teammate Jim Peterson asked, "Does anyone know who George is competing against next week?"

Each of the systems I had experienced so far in college—Kansas, Illinois, Igloi, Lydiard—had strengths and produced great results and success for each coach's protégés, but each plan still left me feeling empty and troubled. What was missing? I had lost my passion. I was still running, and running well, but still I wasn't having any fun. I knew the physical training plans of these highly successful coaches worked, but I was still missing the feeling I had experienced in Morton athletics when I broke five minutes in the mile—in November, at night, alone—on my high school track.

There are various different successful methods for training the physical, as Coach Johnson was discovering. But many lack the benefits from training the physical while additionally tapping into the essence within the mind (Level 2) and the spirit (Level 3). These are the higher levels of coaching that I'd like to address in the next two chapters. It was this spirit (inspirational passion) in particular that I was missing when I first competed in college and that is too often forgotten on athletic fields today. It is a state of mind recognizing sport as play. I hope you will see that this "play" is what I hope to celebrate in this book.

CHAPTER 6

Duality: Mind and Body
(Level 2–Psychology of Coaching, 1970's)

"Confidence is an accumulated feeling attained during
the process of working toward goals, intrinsically created,
that you believe in deep within yourself."

—Coach Al Carius

"I am convinced that letting one's intuitive feelings
guide oneself while also supporting one's teammates in
pursuit of a common goal is far more influential and
powerful in achieving personal bests than competing
against one another. We need each other to maximize
our potential. No one does it on their own."

—Coach Al Carius

Because there were no sports psychology courses at Illinois
in the 1960's, I learned about the relationship between the
mind and the body by taking courses in the Psychology
department. I then related or blended that information with
my Level 1 training in Physical Education. My mentor, Dr.
Glenn Blair, was a professor of Educational Psychology at
the University of Illinois. "Everything a person says or does

is motivation provided to meet basic needs and anyone not motivated is six feet under ground." Edward Thorndike in 1998 suggested his "Law of Effect" principle related to the frequency of our responses to these human needs. He noted that "Responses that produce a satisfying effect in a particular situation *become more likely to occur again in that situation* [emphasis added], and responses that produce a discomforting effect become less likely to occur in that situation." This idea, again, provides a strong case for positive reinforcement of the cultural core values and behavior traits you hope your athletes identify with. I was beginning to understand the connection of the mind to the body in human performance.

During my affiliation with the University of Chicago Track Club under the unrivaled leadership of Coach Ted Haydon, I once attended a club banquet and shared a table with a gentleman who worked with inner-city gangs. In no way am I insinuating that I am an authority on inner-city gangs. However, I do remember what the man at the sports banquet said about the relationship between an athletic team and a gang experience. "A young man can either join an athletic team or a gang, and in each case be satisfying basic psychological/social needs." The satisfaction or motivation for the principle of the Law of Effect is similar.

The human needs met on one path (a sports team, for example) a young man takes can lead to a positive outcome, and the similar needs met on another path can lead to a negative outcome. Thus, I have a very difficult time accepting a school's decision to drop any properly principled, supervised sport. The programs with a solid, positive philosophical foundation will provide a positive, ongoing living experience laboratory to young people, fostering through darkness a guiding light for life—"a means to an end."

The "means to an end" response to the mind-body relationship to life and sports begins with the satisfaction of meeting basic human needs in every situation. Needs determine our thoughts, thoughts influence our feelings, feelings impact our attitudes, and our attitudes stimulate the potential responses within you.

Certainly, the thoughts in our minds have a powerful effect on actual or perceived reality in our lives. Consequently, whatever we want to become we need to create first in our mind and then nurture and reinforce with what we surround ourselves with—what we see, what we hear, what we read, and what we say to ourselves. Self-talk has a powerful influence on what we feel and our attitude toward what we say and what we do. "Nothing is, unless our thinking makes it so," Shakespeare wrote.

Our thoughts are what help us to be human with the freedom to choose our responses in various situations. We tell our athletes that we must train our brain as well as our body in every workout. Similarly, we say that the athlete must first "be" his goal by getting his mind to where he wants his body to follow. Mentally, you are borrowing from the future the person you need to be now. Faith in the future awakens the potential within you. A positive athletic experience provides a healthy environment to nurture these thoughts.

The Hawthorne Effect is a term coined by Henry A. Landsberger when analyzing experiments from 1924-1932 at the Hawthorne Works, a Western Electric factory outside of Chicago. Simply put, Landsberger's study indicated that the environment in which work was being done by workers could have an influence on the effectiveness and production of the workers. In other words, our performance is often influenced not so much by what is taught or said but rather by the atmosphere of the setting in which the teaching takes place. Certainly, this concept has implications for team building.

Back in fourth grade, I remember my favorite part of the school day was story time when the teacher would read a story to us. Keep in mind, this was a regular part of our schedule as a reward for good class behavior. Occasionally as a special treat the principal, Ward Grundy, would be our guest reader. He had a charismatic enthusiasm when he read to us, and through his personality, he possessed the ability to communicate a mesmerizing energy that connected his reading to a sense of reality. Talk about getting our attention! Clearly, our class loved this period and looked forward to that time of the day as a reward for our good behavior. As we periodically discovered, this all changed when our class performance was below the teacher's expectations. "Class, I am very disappointed with you. Today, we are going straight to math with no story time," the teacher would say. And for me, well, I still cringe with the memory of the collective hurt felt by our class at the loss of story time and math as its substitute punishment. What can I say? From that time forward, I froze at the thought of math.

Along the same line, there was a physical education class in which the teacher methodically made a step-by-step case for the importance of physical fitness within our lifestyle. To be fair, the intrinsic value of these activities for the students was presented with great clarity by the instructor. However, the teacher's message about the intrinsic value of exercise was spoiled by his class discipline methodology. For example, the instructor would sometimes say, given the particular situation, "You're late for class, run a lap!" or "You're talking in class, give me 20 pushups!" Making exercise a punishment for misbehavior is unlikely to make exercise attractive to young students.

On the flip side, the atmosphere for learning social studies in my sixth grade class was very different. What could be better than a teacher who fostered passion for a subject? Think about it. We were convinced by this teacher that learning about our past would have ongoing benefits that we could tap into throughout our years of education, thus changing our lives. To no surprise, this teacher's infectious enthusiasm for teaching the material gave us an insatiable hunger for history. In one particular class, he announced we would study Sanskrit literature the following day. Well, that was all we needed to hear because as one could predict, his genuine enthusiasm, facial expressions, and body gestures seduced everyone in the class into anticipating the novel opportunity awaiting us the next day.

In all reality though, not much could be more boring to a junior high kid than this subject matter. Later that evening, my parents asked me what I had learned in school during the day. I moved on from that day's activities quickly to my excitement and eagerness to study Sanskrit literature the next day. Naturally, they said, "Okay, so what is Sanskrit?" I answered, "I don't know, but it must be something very special. After all, one of my favorite teachers was really excited about us learning it!" Hopefully by now you get the idea I'm emphasizing: the depth and speed of the learning process is influenced greatly by the atmosphere, environment, and culture that surround the process. Positive, supportive leadership sets the stage for better learning.

The former Steinmetz coach, Ed Wallace, who we lured to become our jumps coach at North Central College for several years, told me the story of one of the high school athletes he had coached. I will call the athlete "Rick" to make it easier. As the story goes, Ed was trying to emphasize to some of his student-athletes just how important and influential things such as friends, what one hears, what one sees, and one's self-talk are to one's emotions, attitude, and performance. To make that point, Ed decided to test his theory and asked several of Rick's classmates and teammates to participate in an experiment, using Rick as the subject. Throughout one particular day, at the coach's prompting, each person made comments to Rick suggesting that he did not look well. The students regularly asked him, "Was he feeling OK?" Keep in mind that Rick had come to school healthy, energized, and feeling great. However, the accumulated questions about Rick's health status began to wear on him. Rick's initial reaction was to seek a mirror in the bathroom to confirm or reject what his friends were saying.

The day continued like this until practice later in the afternoon. As always, Wallace took his roll at the beginning of practice and eventually came to Rick on his roster. To his amazement, Rick was absent. Concerned because Rick was never one to miss practice, Wallace asked Rick's fellow teammates about him. In summary, a member of the team indicated Rick had progressively felt ill throughout the day and had ultimately left school for home because he was sick. The negative feedback about his health from his teammates ultimately made him *feel* sick.

This concept though—the powerful effect our thoughts can have on actual or perceived reality in our lives—is not new. I remember this story told during my freshman year, in 1960, at Kansas about their legendary 39-year-veteran basketball coach, Phog Allen. (He was called "Phog" because of his powerful, "fog-horn" voice that he employed on the sidelines.) At the half time of games, he had his basketball players each peel an orange in a very specific way, having convinced them that this task would give them extra energy for the second half. Maybe only the placebo effect was involved, but it seemed to work! While Phog Allen coached at Kansas, his teams won 771 games and lost only 233. He retired as the coach with the most wins in college basketball history. It is clear that a coach with the credibility of a history of success will have a hypnotic effect with the words he or she speaks. That coach's athletes will more readily listen to, absorb, and confidently apply the words to their training or races.

Along these same lines, I heard on the radio of a person who was hypnotized, blindfolded, and told a hot iron had been placed on his arm. In reality, it was ice. Improbably as it may seem, the body formed a blister on the spot where the ice had touched the skin. Doesn't that sound super strange and questionable? It surely does to me, but at the same time, extremely interesting and intriguing. The interdependence of the mind and the body have become obvious to me through my years of running, coaching, and life. Our choice to nurture and tap into this mind-over-matter concept can have a dramatic influence on who we are and who we become.

Here's another example from my coaching of the mind's influence within the body. Years ago, I had yet another of my good intentions produce a negative trial-and-error result. I had developed a numbering system which I asked each of our distance runners to use before, during, and after each training session. The athlete was supposed to rate and record how he felt by indicating "fantastic" or "perfect" with a "10" down to "terrible" at the other end of the spectrum with a "1." My objective at the time was for each athlete to mentally read their bodies prior to practice, during practice, and after practice. I thought this information would help me by giving me daily feedback from my runners that I could use to make any needed individual adjustments to the quality or volume of mileage covered in subsequent practices.

I felt this self-numbering system would give a sense of ownership to the athlete and help them read their bodies, thus creating better adaptation to their workouts for them on any given day. Throughout the season, I anticipated that the numbers at mid-workout and at the end would progressively rise toward 10s. To my surprise, ironically, the result was just the opposite of what I had expected would happen as the season progressed, which greatly confused and disappointed me. For most of the team, their numbers declined as the season progressed.

I did not realize what was happening, however, until one of my runners suffered a broken foot. Eric Diekman provided insight into the team's decline in numbers on my charts. You see, Eric was consistently putting his evaluation number at 10 for all three of the check-points. Finally, I confronted Eric, thinking he was making a mockery of my brilliant numbering system.

Curiously, I asked him just how he could possibly be a 10 before, during, and after practice while simultaneously having a broken foot. His answer turned a light switch on in my head. "Coach," he said, "my mind is not broken." He indicated he could not control the fact that his foot was broken, but he could control his attitude towards it. He went on to tell me, "I'm a 10 every day, and I am not going to let the situation with my foot influence how I feel." Talk about the teacher learning from the student! Eric added that each night before he sleeps, he imagines little workmen with hard hats, in his head, and he is sending them down his leg to mend his broken foot! It's wonderful when an athlete can remind his coach, so powerfully, about the importance of the mind on personal performance and wellness.

Eric's is another phenomenal "performance growth" story from a North Central athlete. He placed 136th in the 1996 NCAA Cross Country Championships. Two years later, he won his only college cross country race by winning the 1998 NCAA individual title. Eric had started that 1998 season by stating, "I am going to prove everyone wrong who said I am 'too big' to run cross country." Perhaps Eric's high pain threshold, and his mental toughness, explains in part why he became a national cross country champion.

After hearing the wise insight from Eric, I reevaluated the benefit of my numbering system, realizing that the number each athlete put down *prior* to the workout had a direct correlation on how they felt *during* and *after* the training. For instance, if one of the runners thought he felt like a 3 before practice began, he had a preconceived, anticipating attitude that he was having a bad day and continued with that as his expectation as to just how well his workout was going to proceed.

In my opinion, an athlete's mind filled with positive expectations sends appropriate enhancing impulses to every cell in the body. In contrast, negative thinking inhibits the appropriate impulses from being sent to the active cells and muscles during performance. My point being: the mind, body, and spirit do not operate independently, but must be blended together into a unified whole, and not broken into separate pieces.

116

It's true that physiology and technique combined with talent is a platform from which human performance evolves, but I always felt that a more holistic effect was involved in athletics. We had no sport psychology courses at the time of my collegiate preparation, but I was always convinced of the value of the synergistic blending of mind, body, and spirit in the pursuit of personal bests. In fact, my thesis at the University of Illinois was, "The Effect of Altered Time Cues on the Subjective Feelings of Fatigue and the Pulse Rate." My hypothesis was that the mind's perception of fatigue could be altered by external variables as well as the pulse rate during activity. I believe that athletic training at its best, like education, should include the blending of the various disciplines that holistically create behavior leading to "the knowing."

For example, according to reports, Pete Rose was being interviewed as he was about to break Ty Cobb's all-time hitting record. One reporter asked, "Pete, you need 78 hits to break the record. How many at-bats do you think you need to get 78 hits?" Pete confidently said, "78." The reporter, thinking Pete was kidding, responded, "Ah, come on Pete. You don't expect to get 78 hits in 78 at bats, do you?" Again, Pete answered, "Every time I step to the plate, I expect to get a hit. If I don't expect to get a hit, I have no right to step into the batter's box in the first place. If I go up hoping to get a hit, then I probably don't have a prayer to get a hit. It is positive expectations that have gotten me all the hits in the first place."

This example is not to suggest that positive thoughts alone will create this deepest level of confidence, much less similar great performances. There is no quick fix for great performance. It takes constant training, understanding the concepts, and pursuing your goal with consistency and great patience. Confidence itself is an accumulated feeling attained during the process of working toward goals, intrinsically created, that you believe in deep within yourself. Gaining confidence does not imply that you will *be* the best, but it does indicate that you can be at *your* best.

With this proper state of mind, success—making the most of your God-given talent—is inevitable. It is not wishing, dreaming, or hoping that "something will happen for the best"—it is "knowing." Michael Jordan knew this. Dick Butkus knew this. Pete Rose knew this. Maybe Abe Lincoln articulated it best when he said, "Always bear in mind that your own resolution to succeed is more important than any other."

For maximum benefit for performance, and for the harmony of the mind, body, and spirit, you need an underlying attitude of authenticity and a reinforced will greater than yourself, allowing your servo-mechanism to guide the process toward the desired destination. It is a step-by-step process of overcoming obstacles, gaining confidence, and building momentum that must start with self-discovery and recognizing intrinsic and identifiable goals. You must be yourself. And you must steel yourself with the internal armor of self-discipline. "Without self-discipline, success is impossible, period." Coach Lou Holtz

The great poet-philosopher Ralph Waldo Emerson once stated, "To be yourself in a world that is constantly trying to make you something else is the greatest accomplishment." A friend of mine, Jim Wachenheim, once said this to me on the way to a track meet. I can remember the exact spot and time that Jim spoke those words because they had such depth of meaning to my life at the time. I did not recognize this at the time, but this message had a major influence on me personally and as a coach. Fortunately, the message continues to be a reference point for me while walking the fine-line between molding athletes into a team and not interfering with their individuality.

As an athlete myself, I recognized the importance of self-discovery and learning who you are while competing at the Milwaukee Journal Games Indoor Meet one Saturday in 1962. It is important to note that Jim Beatty, a world-class runner coached by Igloi, had run a 3:59.7 mile in the Chicago Daily News Relays the previous night. Prior to the Milwaukee competition, I was sitting in my hotel room when one of my Illinois teammates called the room to inform me that Beatty was eating right next to him in the hotel restaurant.

Needless to say, I rushed down as fast as I could to find Beatty finishing a full-course roast beef dinner, topping it off with a dish of ice cream. Back then, it was my normal pattern to eat a specific light meal no less than four hours prior to competition. Bolstered by what I saw, I took the risk and ordered everything Beatty was eating. After all, he was at the world-class level and would be competing that evening much earlier than I would. I thought to myself, "What was good enough for a world-class runner would certainly be even better for me."

Well, it all went downhill from that meal on, but not for Beatty. He won that evening in another world-class performance. As for me, well, after my race I dashed straight to the nearest restroom. I was feeling sick to my stomach, wiped out, and was wondering why I was getting a second look at my undigested roast beef dinner. I was unaware at the time of the nervous fight-or-flight response of the body's digestive system that can inhibit the digestive process.

Unsurprisingly, at that moment I realized I was not Jim Beatty. I had to discover more of who I was rather than trying to be someone else. It was a major life lesson and experience that would help me later on as a teacher and a coach. It all begins with getting to know who you are and what fundamental values you believe in. If you don't know yourself, how can you really know and coach anyone else?

Along this same line of thought, there are times in the midst of a workout when I will ask an athlete for his name. While likely thinking his coach's short-term memory has just taken a turn for the worse, he states his name with a very puzzled expression. I ask, "Then why are you being influenced to run someone else's workout?" No *one* workout fits everyone perfectly. I tell my athletes that it is impossible for me to plan the perfect workout for each of our fifty runners and that any coach who says he does has a bit of an ego problem. I also tell them it is important for them to understand the exact concepts of our training, know themselves, and then make the work-out work for them. In order to receive the desired benefit, they need to fine tune the experience to get the specificity from the practice session that will later be transferred to the meet situation. This vitally important idea relates to the importance of specificity.

I also tell my athletes to trust themselves and run their own practice pace so that they can have confidence to "know" how to run their own race when the time comes. Often during meets, athletes attach too much importance to other external variables beyond their control: who is in the race, how many competitors are in the race, the weather, split times, the fans, the noise, the course conditions, the name and importance of the meet, etc. These distractions cause them to lose focus over the things they do control, their attitude and performance on that day, no matter the conditions.

Coach Joe Paterno once said, "Do not ever let anything external to you control you." Clearly, the more an athlete is distracted by outside circumstances, the more that athlete gives his competition (or the elements or the course) the power to control his race. It is key for the athlete to trust themselves from the inside-out, because performance is at its best when one listens to their intuitive signals and is supported by other team members within a cooperative environment. Even for an athlete with much experience, this is an extremely tough concept to understand and implement. This "comparison trap" is one of the biggest obstacles young athletes face today.

I am convinced that letting one's intuitive feelings guide oneself while also supporting one's teammates in pursuit of a common goal is far more influential and powerful in achieving personal bests than competing against one another. We need each other to maximize our potential. No one does it on their own. One reaches his or her highest level and best performances because of all the influences, both good and bad, and all of the positive supporting people in one's life. "Life's most persistent and urgent question is," Dr. Martin Luther King said, "what are you doing for others?"

Resulting from this is the great concept of synergy—the idea that "the whole is greater than the sum of its parts." Synergy within a group creates a truly powerful force and can lead to wonderful performances. Such a combined, focused energy among its members might have been the reason why our "No Name" team of average athletes won our first national championship. My dad once told me that one horse harnessed to a wagon can pull up to six tons of material. In contrast, Dad said two horses working together side-by-side can pull over 24 tons of material. When it really gets down to it, we achieve much more by having faith and trust in each other while working together rather than working separately.

Along with the idea that "All of motivation meets basic needs," I learned the concept of the law of specificity, like many others, from Dr. Glenn Blair, my educational psychology professor at the University of Illinois. He was a former basketball coach who used to say, "You must exercise or practice in the exact way you plan to play in a game." To get an exact result you must exercise in the exact way you wish to compete. This will help your practice experience transfer over and become a natural reflexive habit in real competitions. The great Green Bay Packers coach Vince Lombardi warned us, "Practice does not make perfect, only *perfect* practice makes perfect."

As an athlete, you plan for experiencing every possibility you might encounter in the national championship environment. Often during practice, I will yell out the letters L-O-S and ask the athletes what I am referring to: the Law of Specificity. I want them to be able to remember that we practice specific skills for specific sections of any competition. Clearly, the athlete and team feel much more confident if we have repeatedly worked on visualization, experience relearning, and dress rehearsing the program we plan to implement on meet day.

I had two different basketball coaches during my four years of high school at Morton. One was a science teacher who doubled as the varsity basketball coach. I can look back, not remembering any of the set plays we practiced for the games. Our plays were too complicated. I do not think any of our players really understood them well enough to use them in the games. During games, we were never on the same page because of the complexity of our coach's strategy, and our team play was never really reflexive either because we had too much to absorb and remember.

Since our game plan was overcomplicated, our game play was more like open gym rather than planned, simple, synergistic, and confident competitive responses to the specifics of each moment of each game. One aspect of our practice was shooting free throws. Our coach's thought was that shooting more free throws was the best preparation for our games. At the end of each practice, we were each told to shoot 50 free throws before we could go home for dinner. As a response to our hunger and our desire to go home, we would gather as many balls as we could and rapid-fire basketballs to a teammate to get our shots done more quickly. This didn't make us particularly good free throw shooters.

During my last two years of basketball, we had a very successful basketball star from the nationally acclaimed Bradley University team become our coach. His name was Fred Dickman. He was a master of the law of specificity with his specific simple planning for everything he could anticipate we might face in a game situation. When a situation would arise in a game, we knew exactly how to respond intuitively because of his simple but thorough preparation.

Similar to my first high school coach, he also had us shoot free throws at the end of practice, but he only had us shoot 10. He indicated to us that he was in no rush to go home after practice. The method he taught us was to shoot two free throws in a row and then sprint from one end of the court to the other as fast as we could and then shoot two more, repeating the sprints between each set of two. We only shot 10 free throws, but we had to make 10 in a row to get to the end of our practice and go home. Within these 10 free throws, he had combined the specificity of the skill of shooting, shooting only two at a time similar to a game, the fatigue of running, and the game-like pressure of needing to make each basket—and 10 in a row! That standard focused our attention, and gave us a real incentive to improve our shooting so that we could get home to dinner.

With the law of specificity, in order to get an exact response, you must exercise in an exact way, ideally reproducing the atmosphere as close to the reality of a game as you can. Dr. Glenn Blair indicated in one of my classes with him that he went so far as to have his athletes practice in their game uniforms and having simulated crowd noise within practices.

Occasionally I will ask my students, "What is the best way to develop the strength of the stomach muscle?" I suggest that doing as many sit-ups as possible is the best answer, and then I wait for a response. Predictably, there is agreement with my suggestion, and then I elaborate on the law of specificity, telling them that my trick question was inaccurate and misleading. I tell them that the stomach is a container that catches and digests food and that the more accurate question to ask would have been: "What is the best way to build the strength of the abdominal muscles?" Additionally, I tell them that to build strength it is necessary to do fewer repetitions while progressively increasing the resistance the abdominal muscles must overcome. If you want to build endurance, you should increase the repetitions, but if you want to build strength, you should increase the resistance and not the number of repetitions.

I often will ask recruits about running, "What is the best way to train for cross country or the 10,000-meter run? Is it better to cover eight miles a day or to cover twelve miles a day?" Again, this is a trick question because of the word "cover." Invariably, their answer would be that it is better to cover twelve miles a day rather than only eight miles. Consequently, I bring up the variable of the specificity of the intensity relating to the word "cover" and indicate that I can cover twelve miles a day by walking. Furthermore, I question how well this would correlate to running a cross country meet or a 10,000-meter race. Again, the idea of having the greatest transfer from a practice setting to a competitive setting is to dress-rehearse the specificity of the competitive environment and atmosphere as much as possible prior to race day for physical, mental, and emotional confidence.

Emotional consistency is another very important part of the specificity of mental preparation to be at your best. I believe that coaching the emotional component of being at your best is the area least understood and most left to chance within teams and coaching. For any performance, there is an optimal emotional point that must be recognized and then matched for peak performances. Certainly, this point would vary among the different sports, but in reality, there is an emotional response that is most appropriate for any individual and team.

I tell our team that even the lowest level introductory meet of the year should be emotionally approached in the same way as if it were the NCAA National Championships. Emotional consistency must be maintained throughout the year, even though we will be growing physically, accumulating confidence, and building overall momentum toward "the knowing." Emotional consistency is critical to any athletic performance. Each individual and team must find their "sweet spot," allowing them to most effectively use their God-given physical talents for peak performance.

In a similar vein, the three worst words to say to a team or an athlete are, "This is it," suggesting that the time has come for a top performance. That comment is bound to place undue pressure on your team or athlete. That, at least, was how I felt back in the eighth grade. At that time, during a speech I gave, I said, "Mr. Witzig, it gives me a great deal of pleasure to present the Morton Junior High School this American flag raised up above and these two waste containers."

To this day, I still remember this speech quite well. Unfortunately, I didn't perform well in speaking it that day. I felt so much pressure on me, given that it was a great honor to be asked to make that speech, that I had great difficulty communicating the message while presenting the class gifts to the principal and the school during our eighth-grade graduation ceremony. Fear and the "fight or flight" phenomenon had taken over, creating mental, emotional, and chemical reactions that caused me to freeze emotionally. Clearly, there was a big gap between my practice for the speech, when I wasn't under pressure, and my actual on-stage delivery in front of a gymnasium full of my classmates, their parents, and many friends of the graduating class. I was so nervous and emotional about giving the speech that I went over the peak of my emotional performance curve.

If this seems unrelated to running, here is the connecting thought: emotion, specifically with its control over actions, is a major variable often overlooked in performance, especially in running. Emotion contains valuable stored energy which is what makes it necessary for peak performances. Thus, restraining your emotion during a season, and preserving it during a race, is incredibly important. The optimal amount of emotion to release is neither too much nor too little, but just the right amount—an amount of emotion capable of firing an appropriate response from your nervous system to send the proper number of neuron impulses to the proper number of muscle fibers to get the best possible physical response.

Moving on, let me set the stage for you once again. Whenever I walk slowly through the hall of our stadium and stop to reflect on the 50 years of team photos lining the wall, I am reminded of one of my favorite movies, *Hoosiers*. I love the closing scene showing the picture of the state championship basketball team mounted on the wall of the old gymnasium of Hickory High School. That moment in time at the end of the film captures the team's preparation, experiences, and relationships formed—creating a collection of memories of the process, an invisible bond, and a legacy for a lifetime.

A very insightful part of *Hoosiers* is when the coach, played by Gene Hackman, teaches his young, nervous athletes an important lesson about emotional consistency and staying in the zone of the moment. When Hackman's team from a small town in Indiana makes it to the state championship, the players are overwhelmed by the enormous Butler University field house in Indianapolis, since it is so different from their little gym back home. The coach could see that the players were getting distracted by their external environment and were losing focus because of it.

Reacting thoughtfully, he asked his athletes for a tape measure and proceeded to measure the height of the basket and the distance between the free-throw line and the basket. Confidently, he assured his team that the measurements of the court were exactly the same as those in their much smaller gym in Hickory. Why did Hackman do this? He wanted to show his team that even though the state championship is held in a different city and at an impressive facility, it is still just a basketball game with the same ball and court dimensions, regardless of how different the surrounding environment or atmosphere might be. He was showing up his players' emotional consistency, assuring them that their skills that had brought them to the state championship would work equally well in the huge fieldhouse—whose court dimensions matched those of their small gym back home.

Appropriately, coaches spend a lot of time on the physical preparation of their athletes. Make no mistake, no one would question the importance of consistent and patient development of the cardiovascular system to prepare the body for successful racing. However, here is my suggestion: to add to the process, one should continuously monitor and fine-tune the athlete's emotional approach, to maximize their competitive race plan. For example, as stated before, on my team we treat each race throughout the season with equal emotion regardless of the competition or the perceived importance of the meet. We operate this way under the assumption that accumulated meet experiences help individuals and teams fine-tune their appropriate emotional "sweet spot" in order to be at their best at the end of the season.

Quite frankly, I have seen the negative consequences of doing the opposite, that is, treating the national championship as the race needing the greatest effort—physically, mentally, and emotionally. Too often when a race is built up as unique, as crucial, as larger than previous races, and as bigger than the season, athletes tend to try harder or over-try, therefore interfering with their performance. The truth is, there is a powerful force within positive expectation, relaxing us, enhancing capabilities beyond what we would normally produce, helping us to reach our "sweet spot" emotionally. On the other hand, apprehension and doubt stifles athletes, hindering their performance.

Bob Keck was a good friend and a successful coach at Illinois Wesleyan University. He once told me that if you just do what you have already done *before* you get to the NCAA Championships, you will have excellent results. I now call this the "Bob Keck" rule. As you approach the end of your season, whatever your sport, you do not need to do anything you haven't already done, and you do not need to try harder. *Let* it happen, and do not try to *force* it to happen. In other words, you already "know" that you are ready because of the many success experiences that you have accumulated throughout the season.

With each race experience, we strive to recognize, attain, and guard our thoughts to sustain emotional stability, thus reducing fear of the unknown. Specifically, we practice not allowing our emotions to be altered by externals—who is in the competition, the weather, the course conditions, or the importance of the meet as perceived by other people. This habit is developed by countless dress-rehearsals through specificity training—simulating meet situations during practice sessions. Throughout a practice session, I will yell at particular athletes, "Where are you at in the race?" We concentrate on controlling what we have control over: ourselves.

For instance, winning is an external outcome and often is outside our control. However, our internal battle in the mind and our concentration to run our race to the best of our ability are within our control. Various questions are recognized and evaluated for each practice and each race. For example, what was our level of emotion days before, the morning of, during the warm-up, at the starting line, and during the race? What stressors were felt, and how did they affect performance? What did our best races feel like and why? For these reasons, it is important for each athlete to keep a daily diary recording all the contributing variables and factors that influence how they feel from day to day.

You can understand it would be good to know *why* you feel a certain way during your best performances. Self-awareness of the many variables in your day or week will help you recreate that feeling in the future. One should run for that *feeling* and not for a specific time. Afterwards, you can compare that feeling to the time you actually ran. Understanding as many of the variables that influence performance helps the runner to have confidence in himself or herself, and in their step-by-step process, without overthinking. And focusing on the process instead of the result helps to eliminate fear.

I want our athletes to lose themselves in the race—in each moment and second of the race—running free, instinctively, and automatically and unconsciously dialed into the servo-mechanism leading the way to whatever the outcome may be. Practicing this steady, emotional consistency helps the athlete develop a total composure and a deep confidence, which become important factors in maintaining focus during performances to block out distracting variables faced in the racing atmosphere.

One of our ways to stay focused within the process and "the now" is to concentrate on running the four parts of a race, breaking down the race into smaller parts and check points along the way to the finish line. Part one, for example, is getting position; each athlete must individually work his way to the top third of the field. There is no need to be leading unless your talent is such that you are able to maintain that position through the finish line.

Once you have positioned yourself without over-exerting yourself into oxygen debt, you settle into your part two. Physiologically, you have around seven seconds at the start of the race to push your pace without risking the effects of oxygen debt accumulating. Part two of the race is a comfortable upper-level aerobic state where you are running with mechanical efficiency. Part three of the race is at the half-way point where psychologically the mind tends to lose focus, causing the body to slow down. During part three of a race, our emphasis is to engage the mind to maintain the pace established in part two. The great American miler Ken Popejoy, who held several world records in distance running, was an inspiring assistant coach for our program for many years. He often stated that his best race advice to a runner was to focus on and work this third part of every race.

Most runners slow down during part three of a race, after the half-way point. So, the ability to maintain pace will actually allow you to be passing other runners by holding the pace of part two. Finally, part four of a race is the part near the end of the race where you are able to make a building surge towards the finish line. At times you might witness athletes who are far back in the competition make a mad dash during the final 100 yards, drawing reaction from the crowd. In those cases, the other parts of the race were often neglected and not run properly.

The number one concept that ought to be taught in sports psychology, in my opinion, is to focus on the positive expectation *process* of one's race (or game) rather than focusing on the outcome or winning. I know this might seem strange to most athletes. I mean, is it not important for each athlete to have a goal? Of course it is! However, the goal simply gives the athlete direction and the energy of purpose to take the necessary little steps daily towards achieving the goal. This is again where the goal-driven servo-mechanism becomes so critically important.

It is key to note that the goal *must* be personally generated. It must be felt deeply within the spirit of the self to be classified as, and to have the internal power of, intrinsic motivation. That goal should *not* be presented to the athlete from an outside source. If an athlete is pursuing *someone else's goal,* he or she is unlikely to perform at their best because they will not be able to engage the unconscious, automatic, intrinsic power within this invisible internal force. If the goal is deeply felt within the spirit of the athlete, then the servo-mechanism is triggered and set into motion.

In the movie *The Legend of Bagger Vance,* Will Smith made reference to this force driving you toward success by saying, "Learn how to stop thinking without falling asleep." In other words, being able to turn your brain off without falling asleep will prevent you from pressuring your process with mental overanalyzing and over-thinking. It is often the case where the harder you try and the more you think, the more you are interfering with actually reaching your goal. In the movie, *For the Love of the Game,* Kevin Costner would start his no-thinking focus by clearing the mechanism through the use of "self-talk." Focusing on the process and allowing the automatic goal-seeking mechanism within you to do its work is the best way to approach competition from a mental standpoint. *Let* it happen, and do not try to *make* it happen.

"It's sensational, I didn't expect it. I was just thinking of racing down the course, not of winning. I was not thinking about a medal." These were the insightful words of Olympic Gold Medalist Fritz Strobl, the Austrian who shocked the field in the men's 1.9-mile downhill skiing event during the 2002 Winter Olympics in Salt Lake City, Utah. On top of that revelation, also consider the improbable gold medal won by American speed skater, Chris Witty, in the same Olympic year in the women's speed skating 1,000-meter final. "The gold medal was something I didn't imagine. I didn't feel a thing," Witty said. "It was an effortless race. It was one of those races where you didn't really think of anything, just float." These Olympic athletes were focusing on the process of their racing, not the outcome.

I cannot count how many times I have heard very similar statements like the two above after great performances that just seemed to happen reflexively, instinctively, running by feeling. Contrary to popular belief, great performances are often achieved when the focus is not on a time, on beating someone, on winning, or on any specific outcome really but rather on simply enjoying the experience, being totally engaged in the *process* while at one with yourself and the action. A great example of this for me is watching my 2-year-old grandson playing while moving continually from one activity to the next. He is "in the now." To that end, letting go and losing yourself in the activity while reacting reflexively and instinctively will often result in superior performance. Consider it this way: sometimes trying harder and working harder might not be the best race-day (or game day) approach for achieving personal bests.

I guess this concept sounds a little strange, doesn't it? I have no doubt about it though! On a personal level, I was reminded of the goal I once had of breaking 4:10 in the mile. For the longest time, I tried everything within my imagination to reach that goal, from trying various racing strategies to testing creative training methods. Despite my best efforts, I continued to fall surprisingly short of my goal. The fact of the matter is, I wanted to achieve my goal so intently that I tried to force the desired result. Without realizing it, this actually became a barrier in my mind—an obstacle preventing me from attaining my goal.

My ongoing response was pure bewilderment and frustration, followed by trying even harder and working harder than ever before for this external time goal. At the time, I was in graduate school at the University of Illinois and was running with the University of Chicago Track Club. As previously stated, our club competed in meets with major universities throughout the country. As it happened, we had a dual meet with the University of Wisconsin on one Saturday afternoon. Several members of our club and I traveled from Champaign to Madison, Wisconsin, during the late afternoon on the Friday prior to the track meet. Our late departure for this longer road-trip was due to teaching my classes in graduate school, which prevented me from being able to leave earlier in the day.

As fate would have it, we got lost en route, only reaching Madison at about 1 a.m. Saturday morning. Upon arrival, we had our late-night dinner of hamburgers, french fries, and milkshakes. On top of that, we had arranged to stay at my good friend Mike Manley's fraternity house. I remember sleeping on a living room couch and not getting to sleep until about 2:30 a.m. Later that morning, the fraternity pledges were awake cleaning the house at 6:00 a.m. There had been a party at the house the previous night. Needless to say, I did not get much sleep.

As a part of my pre-meet schedule, my fraternity friend and future Olympian, Mike Manley, and I went to catch up on old times over breakfast off-campus. I was completely immersed in "the now," in the moment, in the present, with no thoughts about the upcoming race in the afternoon. All that was on my mind was just connecting with Mike and the memories we shared as competitors—he at Wisconsin and me at Illinois while undergraduates.

Now imagine this. That afternoon, after all my "poor" pre-race preparation—up late, eating late, little sleep in a strange bed, a long pre-race breakfast—to my amazement I broke 4:10 in the mile for the first time in my life with a time of 4:09.7. Now, I am in no way suggesting the events leading up to the race should be duplicated, nor are they keys to successful performance. But I am convinced my mental approach of disconnecting with the outcome of the race had an enormous positive influence.

Two weeks later, Ted Haydon was called and asked to provide a filler for the NCAA Invitational Mile to be run at the Cobo Hall in Detroit, Michigan. At that point, many prestigious runners from around the United States were invited to race. This list included the great US runner and Olympian Gerry Lindgren. Fortunately for me, the NCAA committee needed one more runner to complete entries for the race. Coach Haydon asked me if I wanted to go.

I was thrilled to be included with such an impressive mile field and to actually have a chance to run on national television. Again, with no thought of outcome, I stepped to the line to enjoy the opportunity. With two laps to go, I was surprised to find myself running effortlessly with the leaders and Gerry Lindgren. Through it all, I was running in the now, in the flow, in the zone, and absorbed with the feeling of an effortless rhythm guiding me to my second consecutive sub 4:10 mile, and ironically, a win.

As odd as it may sound, I again was not focused on a goal but rather lost in the moment-to-moment experience. I approached the race with positive expectation but with no thought of time or place. I was just thinking about running a mile, not of winning. Once again, my point is that sometimes when we are so concerned and distracted with times, winning, and our opponents, we are robbed of the natural intimate harmony available to set the stage for the mindset of doing our best—the invisible world of mind, body, and spirit merged into the moment.

As Dr. Blair noted, our athletes have needs—for personal achievement, for friends (teammates), for recognition. They are thus motivated to create a personal, intrinsic goal—become a better, a good, a great athlete. Working toward their intrinsic goal gives these athletes some of the recognition and friends they sought, satisfying some of their needs. That positive physical and emotional feedback provides them with continuing motivation to work more, or harder, to obtain more satisfaction. Thorndike's "Law of Effect" is thus in motion within the athlete.

If the athlete has good self-discipline, and is perhaps well-guided by a good coach, he may continue this positive feedback loop of work/performance/recognition, and his training and performances become almost automatic. He has learned to improve and to perform by improving and performing. His internal servo-mechanism takes over, guiding him to train and to race toward his intrinsic goal, all the while fulfilling the personal needs that started him down this road of positive personal performance.

This reminds me of the story of Jeff Rouse and "Easy Speed." Jeff Rouse had been the world record holder in the 100 meter backstroke. At the 1992 Olympic Games in Barcelona, Rouse was the clear favorite to win the Olympic gold medal in that event. But sometime prior to the Games, someone had told Jeff that he should be focusing on winning that Olympic gold medal. Despite all of his previous great performances, he came to believe that, to be successful, he must win that Olympic gold. Unfortunately, Jeff instead suffered an unexpected loss in that Olympic backstroke race, taking silver.

Rouse reported later that it took him several years to recover mentally from that loss, and how devastating it had been to him. He took time for himself, and reflected upon the reason he had started swimming in the first place. He remembered that he had begun swimming as a young boy for enjoyment, and liked the feeling of satisfaction he got when he improved himself. He started swimming by losing himself in the feeling of the process while not worrying about the outcome.

Jeff Rouse returned to the Olympics in Atlanta in 1996 with his old attitude, and without a specific goal. He reported that he had been focusing on just being himself and enjoying the process of swimming the backstroke. He said that when he swam like that, he could go at 100% speed with 80% effort. In 1996, Rouse finally won the Olympic gold medal in the 100 meter backstroke.

Make no doubt about it, one must work very hard to get the body prepared to be at its best, and you must be intrinsically motivated. But if this is your situation, then let your internal goal-seeking servo-mechanism take over. Truth is, in most cases, we cannot control what goes on outside, but we can control what happens inside.

Coach Carius's 1st North Central College (NCC) Cross Country Team, 1966

Al Carius (bottom row, center) with University of Kansas Freshman Team, 1960

Kansas Teammates: the great Billy Mills, 1964 Olympic 10k Champion, with Coach Carius

Al Carius at the University of Illinois with Illini Coach Phil Coleman

Coach Ted Haydon, Olympic and UCTC Track Coach—
Al's Mentor and Inspiration

Coach Carius Running with his First North Central Team

1st North Central CCIW Cross Country Championship, 1968

145

Bill Moody, CCI Pole Vault Champion, 1967

1st CCIW Track & Field Champions, 1971, with Coaches Carius & Meinz

147

*Glenn Behnke, long-time Assistant Coach & 1st of 87 Individual
NCAA Division III National Champions, 1974*

The "No Names" with Coaches Carius & Behnke, 1st NCAA National Cross Country Champions, 1975

*New Internal Team Leaders: Jay Rogers, Tony Bluell,
and Bob Dunphey, 1980s*

1st Outdoor Track & Field National Championship, 1989—
Coaches Carius & Gramarosso with Jim Vantlootegem,
Dan Newkirk, & Harold McCadd

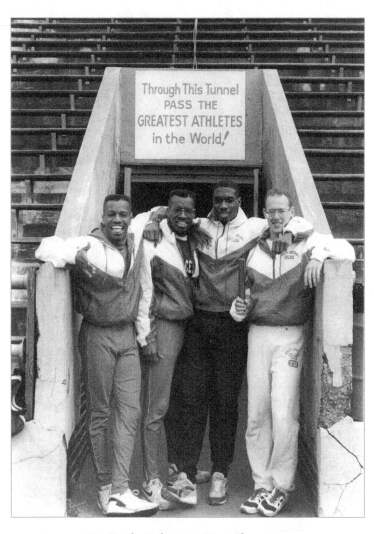

1992 Drake Relays 4x400m Champions:
Gerald McCadd—4x, Harold McCadd—5x,
Andre Coleman—10x, Gale Van Rossem—3x All-Americans

Coach Carius with long-term Assistant Coach Ken Popejoy:
Two Great Runners & Friends, Leading by Example

David Thompson, 2-time NCAA National Champion,
6-time All-American Jumper/Sprinter

Record Low 32 Points & 5 All-Americans for 1993 National Champions Dan Mayer, John Weigel, Brian Henz, Jim Dickerson, Matt Brill, Dan Iverson, Chuck Hof, Rob Harvey & Luther Olson

2000 NCAA Indoor Track, 2nd Place Team, with Track & Field Coaches Tabour, Carius, Winder, Gora, Narayanan, Gramarosso, & Malinsky

4x100m CCIW Champions, 1994 Andre Coleman, Brian Johnson, Joel Badie, Frank Pettaway

Brian Fennelly, 1994 NCAA National Champion
in the Discus

*David Jones, Brian Fennelly, and TEAM! Captures NCAA
National Championship at Home in Track & Field, 1994*

4x100m Exchange: Clint Mobley & Marc Browning

Luke Winder, 6-time NCAA National Pole Vault Champion. His brothers, Josh & Jake, were also pole vaulting National Champions while at NCC

Matt Brill cheers John Weigel to
1995 NCAA Cross Country Individual Title

*Julius White, a Team Leader in the Comeback Years & 5-time
All-American Runner*

Dhruvil (Dev) Patel (658), 6-time National Champion with All-American Teammate Al Baldonado

NCC Packs up behind Mike Spain, 3-time National Track Champion, on the path to the 2009 National Cross Country Team Title

Coach Carius Celebrates with Friend, Colleague, and Successor,
Head Coach Frank Gramarosso

NCC Reclaims the National Championship, 2009. Team with Alumni & Coaches

The Author in His Element

The Stripes

Coach Carius & His Team—Always Coaching, Always Inspiring

CHAPTER 7

The Spirit
(Level 3—Spirituality of Sport, Now)

"A lot of my best never won in high school. They were just dedicated young men who learned how to work for a goal. It always amazes me to hear people pointing out this talent and that talent, when they are simply talking about a boy's physical gifts. The physical is almost minor compared with the heart and desire. I like the character of a man who will suffer to improve."

—John McDonnell, former coach at Arkansas

"The physical and the mental will not survive unless they have a solid foundation. The foundation is the spirit, the character, the attitude that combine to holistically help the athletes to become their best by living consistently with who they are."

—Coach Al Carius

Certainly, the body, mind, and heart have unfathomed influence in sports, helping athletes reach their personal best. But there exists a much more powerful, cohesive force within us, yet not of the physical, which is

171

much harder to explain. It seems to me to be an integrative, omnipotent force coming from deep within (yet originating from a place outside of man) that guides and magnifies the dualistic attributes of the body and the mind within our soul—spirit. Dr. Jeff Duke, in his lectures mentioned earlier, had stressed that athletes might have difficulty sustaining the beneficial effects of the mind/body duality in training without a strong spiritual bedrock to support them.

Throughout my life, I have felt that I have been guided through countless situations transcending understanding, where I would have stumbled had I depended solely upon my own thoughts, actions, and decisions. Spirit is the connection to the sovereign source of truth on earth, providing the light and foundation for the values of character. Spirit is not measurable, but often is observable through our interactions and relationships with others. Faith is the driving force of spirit, and though neither can be seen, they can be felt in the heart.

I must admit there are times when I am very confused as to why things happen the way they do. Some things just don't make sense to me and are as difficult to put into words as a description of air. Air cannot be seen, touched, or held in our hands, yet we know it exists and is critical for us to absorb into our lives to live and grow. I believe we are placed upon Earth with purpose to continually learn, grow, and serve on each day in our journey through life. I am certain that every experience we have and every person we meet in our lives have serendipitous, evolutionary life lessons to teach us, if we keep our minds open and senses alert. Success is not an accident.

The process has purpose, in sport and in life. Not surprisingly, sometimes we underestimate the small, important ways in which our shared moments interconnect to affect the process and the ultimate outcome. When you get right down to it, we make influential differences in our lives each day with the freedom we enjoy to make our own choices of what we think, say, and do. Every interaction has influence, whether positive or negative. We can choose to grow, or neglect these daily signs and opportunities. One of the gifts of being human is choice, the time between a stimulus (situation) and your response.

Some years back, I recognized these inner, spiritually guided relationships in one of my favorite movies, *Grand Canyon*. Seldom have I been so inspired and disappointed during the same movie. You see, I am a big Steve Martin fan and am drawn to any of his movies. I really can't help it—something about him really makes me laugh. Unfortunately, Steve was out of character for me in this movie and did not portray his typical persona—a light and funny image. In fact, the first part of the movie was somewhat dark and depressing. But in spite of my early disappointment, I began to sense in the movie the unseen, controlled Holy Spirit begin to work within the desperate, hopeless lives of the six main characters.

After a series of events and serendipitous encounters, the disorder within the lives of all the characters began to mysteriously interact and to change in purposeful, positive, life-changing ways through a faith not recognizable by the five senses. In *Grand Canyon*, seemingly improbable chains of events guided the right succession of people together for productive, interconnected bonding outcomes. Some kind of higher power was at work in the movie, weaving among the characters, that was beyond coincidence. Yes, this was just a movie. Yet I believe we all, unknowingly, benefit from and contribute to this higher power that affects us and others throughout our lives. It is a gift, driven by the source of an absolute truth. But what is it?

Here is how it works in running. As stated earlier, I became aware of this invisible dimension when I referenced the No Names of the 1975 NCC cross country team, our first national champions. Their motto was, "Our strength is in our inner unity." Clearly, the unbelievable success they enjoyed went well beyond the science of the workouts, their physical talent, and the mental confidence they gained from accumulated experience. Remarkably, on the surface with this team, each individual's physical talent was not proven during prior performances. But science and statistics do not always adequately explain or measure the bonding source of strength teams develop and share through their deeply felt unity. Together, this team had an undercurrent of selfless commitment to one another that could not be measured or explained in any scientific, materialistic manner. Together, this commitment, this invisible force, was created by a supreme being, integrating and synergizing science and faith into the highly implausible result of a national championship.

Here is how it works in life. We are at our best in the support of making a difference in the lives of others and without always realizing that the right people and specific events seem to be guided serendipitously into our lives, amazingly, in purposeful ways. Simply put, everything and everyone seems to have something to teach us and helps us grow. It all has meaning and purpose. For the most part, our choices along the way will determine our direction and destination, as well as how powerful our influence will be in the service of others along our life's path of hills and valleys. "You can't help someone get up a hill without getting close to the top yourself." General H. Norman Schwarzkopf.

Some time ago, while visiting my father-in-law Larry Gregory at Rest Haven Health Care Center, I had the good fortune to meet Johnny Sain. Both Larry and Johnny had suffered strokes and were under the necessary care of the health center. Larry himself, with the support of his loving wife Charmaine, was the most thoughtful, giving man I have ever known. Whenever there was a need in someone's life, Larry was there, offering his help in countless ways. Even though he was now paralyzed on the right side of his body and he could not even talk, he continued to give of himself selflessly with his spirit, enlivening every visitation through a smile, a touch, a gesture, or as best he could, a word, until he passed away on May 6th, 2009.

But Johnny Sain? Does his name mean anything to you? When I met him at Rest Haven, he was confined to a wheel-chair and spent much of his day watching television near where I visited with Larry. Meeting him while visiting my father-in-law seemed mere serendipity. But I as a coach was given the opportunity to meet a professional athlete with a great career who established a remarkable bridge between the old and new eras of professional baseball, and of sports itself. Consider the achievements and the milestones of Johnny Sain's career.

Sain was a Major League Baseball pitcher with the old Boston Braves and a coach on three World Series Championship teams with the Yankees. He recorded three consecutive 20-win seasons and won the first game of the 1948 World Series 1-0 against the Cleveland Indians' legend, Bob Feller. By swapping starts, Sain and his more famous teammate, Warren Spahn, had won eight games in 12 days during the Braves' pennant drive that year. Their two-man pitching rotation in that unbelievable pennant run led to the famous baseball saying, "Spahn and Sain and pray for rain!"

Impressive, yes? But tell me what is more significant in Sain's life and for the game of baseball itself: Sain's great pitching record or the pitch he threw on April 15th, 1947? That day, Johnny Sain helped start a new and long-overdue era in Major League Baseball, the beginning of the end of racial discrimination in professional sports in the US. He threw the first pitch to a batter, Number 42, playing in his first Major League game for the Brooklyn Dodgers, by the name of Jackie Robinson. Earlier in his career, Sain had also helped to end another baseball era, and threw the very last Major League pitch to the famed Babe Ruth.

Was it mere *coincidence* that one single Major League pitcher should serve as a link between those two great baseball eras? Or was there meaning behind the role Sain played? Certainly, there exists another level in sports (and in life) which is much harder to explain than mere pitches and races and games. "If all you see is what you see," the Reverend Tony Evans has said, "you will never see all there is to be seen." Johnny Sain was an amazing and inspiring athlete and coach for this coach to meet. And I was rewarded in meeting him by following an inner voice, visiting my father-in-law at his assisted-living facility.

———

Chances are I may never fully understand the answer to all of my questions about personal performance, but I am convinced we are at our best when we are connecting our body, mind, and heart with the higher power greater than ourselves alone—the spiritual power. Sometimes it is only in the toughest part of the race, and the toughest parts of life, that we realize the holistic, synergistic strength of body, mind, heart, and spirit working in harmony toward exclusive growth and personal bests in serving others in life's race. Sometimes we don't recognize just how important we really are to one another. Jackie Robinson said it best: "A life is not important except in the impact it has on other's lives."

For me as a coach, this is the ultimate goal, inspiring athletes to education through the physical to promote growth of the mind and heart, with the foundational glue of spirit. We are all given great gifts at birth that will ultimately not be defined by a score, a time, a trophy, or a place but rather by the growth and the content of our character, and reflected by our attitude towards others. The great freedom we enjoy is through the choices we can make on a day-to-day basis. Realistically, we are faced daily with powerful influences for both good and bad. It is the spiritual "North Star" within us that, when directed to our soul, gives us the strength of character to choose wisely, to adopt "self love," and ultimately the desire to be of service to others through following this eternal connection from the source of absolute truth.

Everyone on a team has the responsibility and can contribute with their positive energy to this selfless bond of great teams. Let me introduce you to one of my runners, Guthrie Hood. I met Guthrie in 2002 at a basketball game in Merner Fieldhouse. He approached me at halftime and introduced himself as a prospective student visiting the campus via the Admissions department. I was not certain why he had approached me and what he had in mind with the contact. After some small talk about his experience so far on campus through his visit, he asked me about our distance program and expressed his interest in becoming a member of the North Central College running program. Wanting to get more information about him than just his name, I asked, "What kind of background do you have and what are your best times in the mile run?" Guthrie indicated that he had never broken six minutes in the mile run so far in his running career.

My initial thought was that he was not very motivated, and no doubt had a very poor work ethic which would bring nothing of great value to our program. But immediately, I learned a great life lesson: never prejudge a person's heart or spirit based on superficial numbers. Guthrie went on to state that he loved to run, but was born with a congenital deformity of his foot commonly called a club foot. Guthrie stated that he limps with every step that he takes, but has a passion for running.

Immediately, I felt ashamed of myself, and of my initial, superficial, prejudicial evaluation of his commitment and motivation for running as reflected by his subpar mile time. The key word in his communication about running was "love." As quickly as I could, I stated, "It would be great to have you as a member of our distance program."

We communicate to all of our freshmen that they have three ways in which they can contribute and remain a member of our team: 1) performance, 2) attitude, and 3) service to the success of our team. To this day, adding Guthrie Hood to our roster was one of the best decisions I have ever made at North Central College. He became one of the most inspirational (in spirit) runners I have ever had the opportunity to coach. There were times when I would be feeling a bit sorry for myself with my own running performances and would look over to see Guthrie Hood limping along, uncomplaining, and quickly dismiss any self-pity I was experiencing.

Guthrie would finish last or certainly nearly last in most races he would compete in during his four years. But I will never forget the letter of appreciation that Guthrie wrote to me after his first year at North Central College. Guthrie indicated how much it meant to him to have the support of his teammates and coaches even though he had never scored a point for our team. He went on to say that he would do just about anything to have the feeling of placing for the team or at the very best winning a race.

Well, on Saturday, February 14, 2004, Guthrie had his dream come true. Prior to the Carthage College Invitational Track Meet, the Carthage Coach, Stephanie Domin, informed me that only one team, North Central, had signed up for the distance medley relay. She asked if we wanted to scratch our entry since there would be no competition for us. With a big smile on my face, I said that we would run the race.

I quickly made last minute substitutions for our DMR team which included Guthrie in our line-up. Guthrie and his teammates won with a team time of 11:20.60. [Roland Hopkins-1,200 meters in 3:19, Pat Siewert-400 meters in 53.1, Guthrie Hood- 800 meters in 2:32.2, and Patrick Rizzo-1,600 meters in 4:36.2] But, on further consideration, I should say that *we* won. Our entire North Central team won. One young man, running with a painful disability, showed us all a great and ongoing example of running for fun, for the love of the sport. And on this day, he achieved our goal for him—a personal best, his first time winning points for his team. How much more can a coach hope for?

The following fall I had Guthrie Hood in my "Leadership, Ethics, and Values" course which met at 8:00 a.m. on Monday, Wednesday, and Friday. As expected, Guthrie gave his best to every assignment and wrote two lengthy papers for the first part of the course. He sat in the front row and was actively engaged with all class discussions throughout the term. At the end of the term, Guthrie again wrote two magnificent papers for the assigned topics.

At this time, I began preparation for authorizing final grades for the course. I then checked online for the method of recording the final grades. At this point, I was shocked to see that Guthrie Hood's name was not listed for my course roster. I couldn't believe it. Guthrie was not signed up officially for this ten-week course! This would mean he wouldn't have had enough course credits to be eligible to run. Thus, he was most likely ineligible during the entire cross country season, meaning that North Central College had run an ineligible athlete in all our competitions. I could not understand how this could have happened since eligibility is checked at the beginning of each term.

My thought was that a mistake had been made and that God was testing me in that this was a leadership, ethics, and values course I was teaching. This would be a test of *my* ethics and values because now I would have to turn myself in for running an ineligible athlete during the season of competition, which would mean we would have to forfeit our results from every meet. I tried to get ahold of Guthrie immediately to see what might have gone wrong. In between, I made contact with Nick Hurd, a student I had made responsible for taking roll in the course each session.

At this point, Nick informed me that Guthrie already had an overload of course credits but just wanted to take my course for no credit and no grade! He audited my course because he just had an intrinsic desire to learn. So, he had been eligible all year, and my worries about him as an ineligible runner were groundless.

I finally met up with Guthrie. He asked me about taking the two-hour final examination for my course early because of another conflict. I said, "Guthrie, you do not need to take the final exam, you are not even enrolled in the course!" At this point Guthrie said that he would work his conflict out because he wanted the experience he would gain from taking the exam.

What an example Guthrie was, as an athlete and a student, to our other runners and students! And I had nearly rejected him from our team because his times were "slow" in high school. But here was a young man in whom the spirit of which I speak ran wide and deep. What Guthrie had not realized, but what his teammates did, was that he was *winning* in every race that he ran. He was inspired, and inspiring, and continues to be a shining light to countless others on our team and off.

So, what am I trying to say here? How can one contemplate or even begin to explain the mystery of life and our purpose here during our short time on earth? The primary method to understand this unknown is through faith. Faith in an unseen supreme being who had defined our purpose before birth and has surrounded us with clues and signs daily for the path to navigate and influence our choices along the way. Faith? Faith in what? Faith in whom? Faith in the unknown?

What I am suggesting is that faith is a powerful and internal force that feeds us daily with his spirit. This spirit is a living guide to our personal, daily possibilities. Our spirit is what makes us human and separates us from every other living thing on earth. It is the magnet that pulls or rejects the countless influences and decisions that lead us to who we are. And as Carl Jung said, "The privilege of a lifetime is to *become* who we really are."

Faith, openness, and awareness allow us to recognize the whispers, angels, grace, serendipitous experiences, and miracles within our lives surrounding us on an every day basis. It is the intrinsic power deep within us flowing through us. As blood feeds the body, the spirit feeds our soul. "Seeing what cannot be seen. Hearing what cannot be heard. Feeling what cannot be touched." I believe there are many signs throughout life to walk our path with invisible faith and not by sight.

Where is the source? What guides this spirit through our life? Years ago, I was teaching a leadership class at North Central College in the classroom on the second story of the stadium. One of my students, Yonny Mascote, asked me a question that touched me deep within my soul, making me think of the source of this spirit. Yonny, who was also a member of the cross country team, asked, "Why do we equate the word 'team' to 'love' within our program?"

As I began to reflect on my answer, I considered the reason we now always say "Team!" at the beginning of our meetings, at the beginning of practice, and just prior to the start of competition. Each time we unite to say the word "team," it is a time to reconnect to the spirit deep within that cannot be measured but through faith, and helps define who you are.

Allow me to personalize this, and my answer to Yonny, with what I experienced a few years ago while returning home from Lexington, Kentucky, after visiting my sons

Scott and Brent, and three of my grandchildren. Imagine my surprise when along the way between Cincinnati and Indianapolis, on Interstate 74, I saw a sign—Milan, Indiana, Exit 156. Words do little to describe the excitement and anticipation that struck me at the time. It is not often we have the opportunity these days to go back in time into history. In light of this, instead of focusing on getting home, I took a right turn at Exit 156 and a left turn down a winding two-lane Route 51 that led me south 12 miles through several really small towns alongside cornfields and eventually to Milan, Indiana.

The simple truth is we all take important detours from time to time through life. Admittedly, you might ask, "What is so big about a small town in the middle of Indiana?" The fact is, Milan, Indiana, is the home of the tiny school that beat the giant Muncie Central for the Indiana State High School Basketball Championship in 1954. This town of 1,150 people, this school of 67 boys, and this state high school championship game played at Butler University in Indianapolis in 1954, was the basis for Hickory, Indiana, and the movie *Hoosiers*. It's my favorite movie for reasons very personal to me.

As I found it, for the most part, there was not much to Milan, Indiana. In fact, for anyone not familiar with its storied past, the town's one-block-long Main Street would remind them of a vacant ghost town with most of the businesses gone or storefronts boarded up. As far as I could see, the only reminder of this David versus Goliath basketball story was an old rusted water tower surrounded by weeds with the fading painted message: "State Champs 1954."

Nonetheless, despite all of the desolation I found in the downtown area, I was mesmerized and sentimentally united with the community that produced this basketball dream story and everything surrounding it that took place in 1954. Ah, for the good old days! It was a much simpler time. As odd as it may seem, I felt at home there and spent the better part of the day wandering around, taking pictures with my cell phone, and talking to people until my cell phone battery went dead.

Throughout my visit, I focused on finding the connection, the look, the feel, and the emotion of the town. I wanted to attribute what had taken place all those years ago to what I could see and feel, and find any clue to revive the landscape of the historical conditions of 1954 Milan, Indiana. For me, the feedback was overwhelming.

Given this feeling, I chose to stay as long as possible, soaking up the history of the town and the team that gave us this wonderful story. But, by the time I arrived back in Naperville that evening, I had taken so much time reminiscing that my family was concerned and was praying for my safety, ready to call the State Police since they could not reach me through my dead cell phone. Sometimes, even taking meaningful detours in our lives can cause us short-term trouble!

Back to the reality of my detour. So, what is the relationship for me between that little town of Milan, Indiana, "team," and "love"? What is their connection to "spirit"?

First let me say that, maybe obviously, I felt a connection between the Milan, Indiana, basketball champions of 1954 and our own 1975 No Name national champion cross country team here at North Central College. No one but the coach and the members of each team expected them to perform as well as they ultimately did. Both sets of teammates *believed* they could be champions before they achieved that goal. As well, I have felt that Naperville, Illinois, when I first arrived there back in the fall of 1966, was very like Milan, Indiana. Though Naperville has prospered and grown, and Milan has not, the similarities at the time—two small country towns where time seemed to stand still—were very significant and real to me.

Second, during the team huddles in *Hoosiers,* the players put their hands together and yell, "Team!" After seeing the movie for the first time, with my son Scott, I changed our collective "yell" at NCC to "Team!" to reflect the faith and spirit of those small-town *Hoosiers* athletes, represented by that word, that team cheer. From that time on, I indicated to our athletes that "team" is not merely a word but a deep, connecting force felt within—and felt between teammates—that arises from an invisible higher power, love.

But back to the classroom and Yonny Mascote's question: "Why do we equate the word 'team' to 'love' within our program?" As I reflected on my answer, I began to cry for the first time, and the only time, during one of the countless courses and classes I have taught during my 50-plus years of teaching. My subconscious mind had made a connection between Yonny's question and my Father's funeral at the Apostolic Christian Church in my hometown of Morton on May 8th, 1985.

At that funeral, the Reverend Bob Phederer spoke of the source of my father's great love of life, family, friends, and people. At that time, the Reverend said that the only source for my father's love could be from the spiritual source of God. My father's purpose and meaning in life, as well as my mother's, came from knowing God in the deepest sense, and reflecting this love throughout their lives. I believe my father's life was a reflection of Corinthians 16:14—"Let all you do be done with love." He stressed to me repeatedly, "If you are in a position to help someone, and you don't, you ought not be in that position." My mother, too, taught me another significant life lesson. "Sometimes in life you only get one chance to do the right thing."

I hold these lessons from my parents very close to me, and they, along with the examples my parents set for me, have guided my work for 50 years as a coach and an athletic director and a professor. I take C. S. Lewis's statement to heart: "Human history is the long terrible story of man trying to find something other than God which will make him happy." After regaining my composure in the Leadership, Ethics, and Values course, I shared with my class the connections I felt between Milan, Indiana, *Hoosiers*, "team," and "love."

North Central College has been *my* Milan, my Hickory High School, my Morton for the past 50-plus years. I am a Christian, and the spirit of the all-mighty God growing through my faith in Jesus Christ has been the heart of my coaching philosophy and, in my opinion, the reason for our success. Our success was based not solely upon my Level 1 coaching and knowledge of the science of the body, or just on an understanding of the dualism of Level 2, the mind and the body, but on a goal of focusing on and adhering to Level 3—the spirit. The physical and the mental will not survive unless they have a solid foundation. The foundation is the spirit, the character, the attitude that combine to holistically help the athletes to become their best by living consistently with who they are. "I certainly believe," the actor Lawrence Fishburne attested, "that being in contact with one's spirit and nurturing one's spirit is as important as nurturing one's body and mind. We are three dimensional beings—body, mind, and spirit."

Reverend Don Borling, who is the minister of the All Saints Lutheran Church in Orland Park, has become our team's spiritual coach through the years, after his son, Jeremy, attended and ran for North Central College. Often, I would have him speak to my Leadership, Ethics, and Values class, since I firmly believe that a solid spiritual foundation in our life helps us to navigate through life and its challenges along the way. At times, he would explain that there was a difference between religion and spirituality. It has always been difficult for me to understand why there were so many different religions when the goal of all should simply be following the direct line of communication from the source of absolute truth, God's word through the spirit of Jesus. My own conclusion is that the many different religions provide us with numerous paths and choices, with different road maps to the same end. The ultimate goal, turning through faith to the source of the Holy Spirit, is to feed the soul by following God's spirit through submission to his son, Jesus Christ.

Again, in his book on the three levels of coaching, Dr. Jeff Duke made a direct reference to one of my favorite movies of all time, *The Legend of Bagger Vance*, and the game of golf. Dr. Duke states that Junuh, the main character in the movie, evolves in the movie through these three levels of philosophical development as he tries to find his soul, or his "authentic swing," the one he was born with. Adversity in life had affected Junuh and he lost his "swing," or his knowledge of who he was. Throughout the movie, Junuh struggles to regain his swing through practicing, at the measured Level 1, by hitting more golf balls or trying harder on the physical level.

At this time Bagger Vance, who I would label an angel sent from God to help Junuh, enters Junuh's life to help him find his swing. "How do my hands have to be? What do my hips have to do? How do I hit the ball a certain way?" Junuh asks. But Junuh fails because he is dwelling on the demons of adversity within his life. This internal battle cannot be won alone and needs the intervention of the angel—Bagger Vance.

Bagger helps Junuh learn that his swing isn't something that can be found solely by physical means. Junuh must go to a higher level and blend the mind and body together in the present moment, in harmony with the surroundings and the feeling of being in the zone or the now. Bagger puts this Level 2 evolution into the best words when he describes this feeling as "How to stop thinking without falling asleep." It involves not focusing on the *outcome* of what you are doing, but losing yourself in the *process* of the game and enjoying the experience.

Finally, Bagger helps Junuh overcome the emotional physical block in his life, caused by previous pain and adversity, that has been limiting his growth. Deepak Chopra described this type of win over oneself this way: "In the process of letting go, you will lose many things from your past, but you will find yourself." Bagger makes Junuh realize that he is not the only person who has a burden on this Earth; others have adversity and burdens that they face and carry. But it is time to let his pain go and not be controlled by the past. It is in this moment of the inspirational talk from Bagger that Junuh finds his true self again, his "swing." He recognizes the analogy to life that, "Golf is a game that can't be won, only played." The goal is to be the best that *you* can be in competition with yourself. Yet the competition is *with* yourself but not *by* yourself. Bagger ultimately tells Junuh, "You ain't alone… I've been here all along. Now play your game… the one that only you was meant to play… the one that was given to you when you came into the world."

Golf is an analogy for life in the same way that a cross country meet is for life. Cross country and distance running are not linear experiences with a simple start and a finish. You are challenged by many obstacles along the way—hills, rain, snow, wind, temperature, turns, soft ground, and hard ground. Through all of it—good and bad workouts and good and bad races—it is important to run *your own race* from start to finish. You run with the foundation of your training of the physical and the benefit of the Level 2 mental servo-mechanism. You must "Find your swing," "Run your own race," from your rock-solid spiritual substructure.

You run with the integration of the body and mind from this internal, "knowing," spiritual foundation of truth. You were put on Earth to be the best that *you* can be with the gifts from God and His spirit lighting the way, to be *our* best through our freedom of choices while enjoying "Fun and Personal Bests" along the way. After all, this is how authentic success on Earth is really measured. And where does the inspiration (in spirit) come from? For me, all answers in life point to the all-knowing, never-changing word of God.

God connected heaven and earth by sending his Deity to earth as man through his son, Jesus Christ. Christ died on the cross for the sins of mankind, and arose three days later to show us the way to everlasting life. His spirit remains available for everyone, to choose to live following God's absolute truth via the spirit of Jesus, or the situational laws of man. Again, God's spirit is the foundational glue for the mind and body, in life and in running.

Jesus lived 30 years of his life as a carpenter. But no one ever talks about his physical woodworker creations. In contrast, Jesus dedicated only three years sharing his word on earth along with his disciples. What continues to be more enduring, his woodwork or his spirit within humanity?

In my opinion, Coach Doug Bruno shared the correct goal with me when he said that our job as coaches is to pass on to the younger generation the eternal values that helped make our country great. I believe it is our responsibility to share these truths in our home, churches, schools, and, yes, within our athletic programs.

CHAPTER 8

Team!

"Through the years, it became clear to me that the
secret to success at North Central was not in the
formula of our workouts but rather in the attitude of
the individuals and their ability to blend selflessly into
a team sharing a common goal."

–Coach Al Carius

"Five players on the floor functioning as a single unit.
Team! Team! Team!—No one more important than the
other."

–Coach Norman Dale, *Hoosiers*

"No individual is bigger than the team.
Anybody who thinks they stand alone needs
to have their head examined."

–Coach Al Carius

I once heard this feedback from a distance runner prospect
who was considering coming to North Central College.
A coach from another college he was considering told
this athlete: "Don't go to North Central. They place more
emphasis on the team than on the individual." My proud

answer to him was, "Yes we do. And that individual athlete will become much better when he is part of of a team."

Only seven runners make up a "team" in a scored cross country race. But we call the rest of our team our "8th man" because of the incredible support they provide and the positive synergistic effect produced when they are running with the top seven or supporting them along the course.

Cross country is a great team sport, in that each of seven participants in a scored race specifically influences the final score. Every runner's performance, and his specific place in the race, counts. Here is where the team's trust in each individual teammate, and the personal performance of each athlete, comes into sharpest focus.

Possibly our best example of the importance of each individual performance for our team as a whole came in 1997 during the NCAA Cross Country Championships held at Franklin Park in Boston, which had been the site of our first National Championship in 1975. Understand that only a team's top five runners are counted in the team score—and the lowest score wins—but runners number six and seven on a team "push back" every runner from another team that they finish ahead of. The better your sixth and seventh runners run, the higher the scores of the runners from other teams who finish behind them.

In Massachusetts that year, Mount Union College had a great team, as usual. Their top five runners placed 2nd, 3rd, 6th, 12th, and 73rd. North Central's top seven placed 7th, 9th, 24th, 26th, 28th, 29th, and 51st. So our sixth and seventh runners both placed ahead of Mt. Unions' fifth runner, and "pushed back" his place by two points, from 71st to 73rd. We won the national title that year with a score of 94 to Mt. Union's 96, thanks to the two points our sixth and seventh runners added to Mount Union's score. Talk about the importance of each individual athlete to the team! It's important to remember as well that cross country is not track—the meets, though of the same distance, are run on courses that can vary dramatically—and so race times mean little in cross country. Young runners in particular should realize from this story that you don't have to be the fastest runner on your team to have a profound and positive effect on your team as a whole.

Whenever we win a team award, we present it to one individual team member to honor and recognize the positive behavior he has modeled for the entire team that year, or in that meet. We make it clear that this individual did not win the award by himself. It's just a reminder to him, and a lasting memory for all our athletes, of all who contributed to win that award. This practice I again attribute to my mentor, Ted Haydon. Ted told me that trophies get lost in a closet or a trophy case just gathering dust. But, in the possession of individual team members, those trophies can have lasting value to the individual and his teammates by highlighting the importance *to the team* of the virtue he displayed during the season. We believe that this private, team-only award ceremony helps to reinforce for our athletes the importance of these individual virtues to our team.

I can think of many stories when I consider the awesome teamwork required for the consistent success of teams within and outside sports, and how the individual is better because of the team. The first is a story of a great football running back who was a star at the University of Illinois. Week after week he was interviewed after each game and personally took all the credit for his great rushing statistics in that game. Finally, his teammates, particularly the members of his offensive line, had heard enough. They decided to "lay down" during the next game and see how well the star running back did on his own. Needless to say, the star had no success on his own that week. He got the message, and realized his accomplishments were dependent upon the strength of one unit working together rather than one star working alone.

The second story is from Carl Poelker, a good friend and an outstanding national level football coach while at Millikin University, within our own college sports conference. Carl told me, "One of the toughest things to do in football is to move the ball into the end zone when you are in the red zone," less than 20 yards away. To move the ball and score, he said, "The players must believe in their teammates, they must believe in their system, and they must believe in themselves." If these beliefs are not real, and felt deeply within the players themselves, their chances of getting into the end zone and scoring are greatly diminished. But that success begins with knowing, and believing in, yourself.

Sydney J. Harris, the prolific long-time columnist with the *Chicago Sun-Times,* explained the importance of self-knowledge and self-respect this way: "Ninety percent of the world's woe comes from people not knowing themselves, their abilities, their frailties, and even their real virtues. Most of us go almost all the way through life as complete strangers to ourselves—so how can we know anyone else?"

Track & Field, with 21 events, has provided us with countless examples of individual performances being magnified and synergized by connected team energy. Each event is a sport by itself with a diversity of typical personalities, skills, rules, techniques, and equipment. Because of the many differences among these 21 events, it is very difficult to create a unified team feeling as one might in basketball, for example, where five teammates play together at the same time with one basketball. However, this diverse group of events and athletes can be bonded together when given a shared, agreed-upon common purpose. So it is very important that coaches and team leaders work diligently and constantly to build such a team feeling among the athletes in all the different track and field events who may never actually train together, or even see each other except on meet days.

Traditional competitive team rivalries are often a great way to stoke such team-building unity. I often state how thankful we are for the many other great teams we compete against at the state and conference levels. Their great competitiveness helps us to be ready to be at our best. With that common purpose, with a genuine brotherhood of love, and great competition, individuals can elevate their performances to near-miraculous levels of outcome. In my experience, most unusually enhanced achievements don't take place when one is competing for oneself. They primarily occur when there is a connection to something bigger and more significant. Competing with teammates with unity of purpose against a respected, worthy opponent creates the best environment for the individual to be at his best.

Here are some stories about our own track & field athletes growing to know themselves, and contributing their very best performances to their teams. They have produced so many great team stories for us over the years, it's hard for me to mention only a few. Remember that track & field is somewhat of an odd "team" sport, since in most events (except relays) each athlete is performing as an individual within his or her event, but trying to score points *for the team*. These stories show how some of our North Central track and field athletes learned to "get it" over the years, and produced some outstanding and often selfless performances for their team.

In 1979, our Jim Nichols had been injured during the entire outdoor track season, until the CCIW Conference Championship meet at Illinois Wesleyan University. North Central was considered an underdog that year in comparison to the excellent Augustana College team coached by the legendary Paul Olsen. Year after year, North Central would battle one tough Augustana team after another for the team title, and this year was no different.

In hindsight, it seems clear that this long-standing team competition inspired Nichols for this meet. He raced his first 800-meter race of the season that day, against stiff conference competition, and amazed us all by coming away with a victory! There's no question in my mind that his performance was energized and synergized beyond his normal physical and mental performance. Something bigger than mere effort was at work within him. And Jim's outstanding, selfless race after his long injury helped elevate the rest of his team to overcome the odds and claim an unexpected team title.

At another CCIW conference championships in 1983, on a blistering hot Friday night, our Tony Bleull was racing in the 10,000 meters against North Park College's Dave Valentine, the previous national champion in the event. Bleull developed horrible blood blisters that hot evening while still running Valentine off the track and winning the event for North Central. Many runners that evening also suffered terribly from the unusual heat.

The following day, despite his bloody feet, Bleull came back and *requested* to double in the steeplechase—a race he had *never competed in before*—in order to try to win points

to help his teammates win another conference championship. Bleull took second in the steeple to add more points
to North Central's winning margin that year. That's a teammate, giving his all to support his fellow teammates.

Two similar outstanding individual performances
helped North Central to its second-ever outdoor national
championship in track and field in 1994. Brian Fennelly,
from Maine South in Park Ridge, Illinois, was one of our
great throwers. As an incoming freshman, he told North
Central's throws coach Pat Gora that he wanted to focus on
the discus in college, and give up throwing the shot as he
had in high school. In fact, Brian did become the Division
III national champion in the discus in 1994, as a senior, with
a throw of 170 feet 3 inches. But he was so good that his
win in the discus was not unexpected that year—he threw
six feet farther than the second place athlete. North Central had counted on his discus win going into that national
championship meet.

Luckily for Brian, and for us, Coach Gora had talked
with him his freshman year and encouraged him to keep
working on the shot put as well. Gora convinced him that he
was too good in the shot to simply give it up. That coaching,
and Brian's resolve, kept him working on both the discus
and the shot for four years. In the weeks leading up to that
1994 national meet, Brian was ranked 16th nationally in the
shot and, to limit costs, only 15 athletes were allowed by the
NCAA in each track and field event. But Brian Fennelly was
given a waiver to compete in the shot put that year because
he had already won a spot at nationals throwing the discus.
Brian dug deep for his teammates at nationals and finished
in sixth place in the shot put, up from his ranking at *16th*,
and won more points for his North Central teammates.

And how much did all his extra work on the shot for four years, and the few extra points he thus won at nationals, mean for his team?

North Central's David Jones was a triple jumper in 1994 and, like Brian Fennelly, proved at that national meet what it means when an athlete rises, accepts the challenge of *outperforming*, and comes through for his team. For some reason, the triple jump competition dragged on till the end of the meet that year, essentially becoming the last event. Traditionally, an exciting and often tight 4 x 400 meter relay race is the final event of a track meet, and may prove to provide the winning team with their margin of victory. On this day it was to be the triple jump which would decide the outcome of the meet.

Our David Jones was sitting in sixth place, with three jumps left. Our team was sitting in second place, a few points behind the team from the University of Wisconsin—LaCrosse. And for some reason, that great LaCrosse program did not have a competitive triple jumper at nationals that year. Our jumps coach, Doug Malinsky—another of our great assistant coaches—realized as I did that Jones had a chance to win the meet for us, if he could dig deep for one more personal best. If Jones rose to fourth place with one of his jumps, North Central and LaCrosse would tie. If he jumped his way into third place, North Central would win.

Coach Malinsky reviewed the situation with David Jones, who asked him "How much farther do I need to jump?" Malinsky pulled out a sheet of paper and drew an eight-inch line on it. "This far," he said. Jones, showing great pluck, replied "Is that all?"

By this point, most of the athletes left at the meet, and certainly the teams from North Central and LaCrosse, understood that the triple jump held the key to the meet. You can imagine that our other North Central athletes and home team fans—NCC hosted the national meet that year in Naperville—were shouting and hooting in support of their triple-jumping teammate. Jones took the first of his three remaining jumps, and fared no better. He took his second run and hopped, skipped, and jumped to a personal best of 48 feet 8 1/2 inches! Our team and the crowd roared as they realized David had moved himself into third place. He stayed there after his third and final jump, and earned the winning points for the NCAA National Championship for his teammates. North Central 75, LaCrosse 74. Brian Fennelly's extra points in the shot put moved NCC in reach, and David Jones's extraordinary leap to a new personal best put us over the top. Two great examples of individual performances being magnified and synergized by connected team energy. They helped to show the power of "Team!" in the achievement of great individual performances.

Every athlete has something to contribute to a team, whether it is great individual performances like those described here, personal bests, positive attitudes, or just joy and humor. Every personal best makes a track & field or a cross country team better, step by step, just as every point an individual can earn for his or her team can be *the* winning point. Our great event coaches and I recognize this. We do our best to show our athletes how they can contribute to their teams by making the most of their God-given talents as they achieve their own personal bests.

My final team story is from within our own North Central cross country team. To me, it is an amazing ongoing historical record of the power of team building. Every summer since the mid-1970s, we have had a team picnic that features a Varsity vs. Alumni volleyball game. During all those years, the team of Varsity athletes has only beaten the Alumni team once—in 1989. It rained on the day of that picnic, which kept the Alumni numbers down. Now understand, we don't play volleyball except on that one day each summer, but the older and (generally) less fit Alumni team *always* wins. What can account for this amazing streak?

Youth, fitness, and numbers annually favor the Varsity team, which includes any freshmen who make the event. The Alums, alternately, seem to rely on a cohesiveness built upon their wisdom of the past, basic concepts, values, and intrinsic feelings they share. They learned, practiced, absorbed, and integrated these strengths during four years of building the life skills of trust, loyalty, pride, and the "knowing" within "team." It doesn't matter that many of the Alums playing volleyball were not direct teammates and may not even know each other. It is a random sample of Alumni who show up each year. Their team bond is nevertheless internal, and eternal.

In contrast, the Varsity and freshmen always struggle to connect, to capitalize on their physical abilities while matched against the unity of the Alums. This team unity or chemistry among the Alumni, and the communication skills that come with it, takes time to develop. It is, frankly, like love.

In my opinion, there is no love at first sight any more than there is an automatic "team" bond when you put a group of individuals together on a roster. Great teams take time to develop the internal attachments which connect them into a synergistic force. One of the key factors in that force, developed over time, is the sense of trust that exists among teammates—the knowledge that you know your teammates will always be there for you regardless of the difficulty. You can count on him and he can count on you. I like the saying from motivational speaker Jim Rohn, which defines a perfect attitude among teammates: "I will take care of me for you, if you will take care of you for me." When you step to the line and look to the left and to the right, our great runner and long-time coach Glenn Behnke said, you "know" you are prepared and you "know" your teammates are prepared and are running for each other. When this has developed, when it is real, a positive expectation collectively exists within each runner on the team, within each player on the court.

I think often of the 45-year history of this summer volleyball match. I remember all the alumni who have played through the years. I think about the fitness and youth advantages of the Varsity, and I recall the single Varsity victory in *1989*. I think about how this is about much more than volleyball, and the great lessons learned. And then I remember what is most important about these annual matches.

The experience is not about volleyball. It is not about selfishness. It is not about who made the best serves or who scored the most points. It's not about who made the best sets or who hit the most spikes. It's not about who clapped the loudest, who yelled the most, nor even about the final score.

Each year, the Varsity group have a few who have the accumulated, experiential "blueprint," with others still discovering the unifying feeling. The freshmen cannot share the deep connection yet because of a lack of common experiences. The Varsity would *like* to do well, and give their best physically, but as a group do not yet possess the genuine glue of love for one another, and the interconnectedness, that the Alumni have. Not every alumnus of NCC's

Track & Field and Cross Country program has this reaction in their heart, but each one who chooses to return to the picnic "knows" it because they remain connected to their roots here in our program. The Varsity would *like* to do well, but the Alumni *know* and *expect* to do well.

"The Varsity would like to win, but we know we will win," Alum David Slinn confirmed. This "knowing" the alums share does not occur automatically by going out for the team. It comes about through a law of life: The more you give, the more you get.

This knowing, like a team, develops over time—during brutal hill workouts at Blackwell Preserve and the old ski hill at Four Lakes, during two-hour runs and intervals and tempo runs together, during morning runs in the rain and snow, the cold and the Midwest winds, and during disappointments and adversity. When you cross-train by yourself while injured, answer the alarm early every morning while other students are sleeping, help a struggling teammate through a race, and don't care which of your teammates crosses the finish line first. When it's summer and thoughts of your commitment to your teammates gets you out on the roads, and you fight through the tough part of a race and finish remembering the many times you put your hands together and said, "Team!"

These are the challenges, and the gifts, of being on a team. It's much more than just working out together physically. It all begins with trusting and knowing yourself, which then transfers over to understanding and trusting your teammate. Trust, from the coach and among the teammates, is the basis of all great teams. Coach Phil Jackson taught and showed us that. We stress the power of "Team!" here at North Central, and the practice has served us very well.

You learn from every experience both good and bad. One of the more painful experiences of my life, as I have noted, was the one semester I spent at the University of Kansas. Again, I was very immature and naive when leaving the well-defined security of my hometown of Morton. Yet Coach Bill Easton at Kansas was a highly successful track and cross country coach whose influence still helped shape the philosophy which evolved into North Central College Track & Field and Cross Country. He also taught me how little details can have profound influences on outcome.

For example, Coach Easton had designed two cross country courses which he would use for home field advantage during dual meet competition. If Coach Easton felt that the visiting team was primarily made up of middle distance, speed-type runners, he would run the competition on a very hilly course which he knew would be detrimental to their performance because of their lack of basic aerobic strength. However, if Coach Easton felt that the competition was a strength/slow-twitch team dominated with 10,000-meter runners, he would choose to run the race on a very flat, fast course to minimize their advantage on the hilly course. There are often two types of distance runners in cross country, those who love hills, wind, rain, snow, and mud, and those who love flat, dry courses. Those who love hills are very strong but often lack speed. You could call Coach Easton's two courses "Making the most of your home-field advantage."

I can't say that I ever attempted to give our North Central runners such a home-field advantage in cross country. But the one thing Coach Easton did that had a dramatic positive effect on our program at North Central College had to do with his choice of uniforms for competition. You see, back in the 1960s, there was no such thing as automatic timing. All the judging and timing at finish lines was done by a group of officials who would pick and time one of the finishers in every race. Needless to say, this would often be extremely difficult if not impossible in some of the shorter races like the 100-yard dash. Eight lanes and eight athletes crossing the finish line at times seemingly side by side often caused a great deal of confusion and mistakes that altered the individual places and ultimately the final team scores of meets.

Coach Easton thoughtfully planned to have his Jayhawk athletes stand out better and be more visible at the finish line by designing a uniform with a pink top and powder blue shorts. True to his thinking, the Kansas runners were more noticeable than the more traditional team colors of red, white, blue, and green. I thought this idea was ingenious at the time and gave his athletes a better chance at being picked correctly at the finish of a race.

I brought this concept to North Central College in the fall of 1966 and implemented it within our program for the first time in the fall of 1968. I wanted our athletes to be unmistakable from the other runners in cross country competition, for a number of reasons. The fall of 1968 was the first time our cross country team began using our red and white candy-striped uniform tops. The idea was to have a very distinctive top that could be easily picked out from among several hundred other runners in big invitationals and the NCAA National Championship.

Our candy-striped racing jerseys gave us a visible distinction, and are an advantage for our competing athletes hoping to be able to spot and run with teammates in a crowded race. They also help all of the fans who are in attendance watching the competition. Through the years, these striped shirts evolved from being a practical visual advantage in competition into a much deeper psychological and spiritual strength for each athlete earning the right to wear the jersey during the three championship meets at the end of our season.

We have a special ceremonial meeting one week prior to the conference meet in which we have one of our numerous alums speak to the team and present each member of our team his striped jersey to wear during these championship meets. The selected alum will represent our storied history and every North Central College athlete who has ever worn the striped top. At this time, the receiving athlete is reconnected with the celebrated success behind the stripes. Our ceremony, we hope, moves our young athletes from recognizing the superficial distinction of our red and white striped top to a deeper energizing expectation of success, based upon the hundreds of North Central College runners who have represented themselves and our program from 1968 to the present.

The best explanation of the symbolic significance of our candy-striped uniforms within our program is presented in an essay, which I reprint here, written by NCC alum John Weigel. Weigel, a great North Central runner himself, discusses our tradition of wearing our red and white striped jerseys each year only for our conference, NCAA Regional, and NCAA National Championship competitions, which we label the Championship Stripe phase of our season.

When John Weigel received his striped top for the first time, he asked to have the one that appeared to have shown the most wear because he felt that more of our alums would have worn that particular jersey through the years. For John, the jersey represented tradition and values much more significant than the unique look of the candy stripes themselves.

We think John expressed the power and the importance of these team traditions very well in a series of articles he wrote for his teammates, "Behind the Stripes," "One Winter Monday," and "Senior Day at Lincoln Park." You can read them at the end of this chapter. His stories may come across as a bit too much, a bit too chauvinistic, for readers who are runners on other teams. But as a coach, can you blame me for treasuring this view from my runners' perspective? It is wonderful to hear back from our runners the ideas and ideals that we have worked to teach them.

I know, we coaches know, the value and the energy that our athletes gain from the support within their teams. Positive, supportive teammates are of immeasurable value to a team as a whole, and to the individuals who make up the team. Just as the team grows stronger athletically with the achievement of every individual personal best, so the team grows steadier emotionally, and in spirit, through the year-round mutual encouragement of each teammate for the others.

The great NBA basketball coach, Phil Jackson, once noted that it was actually his job to become "an invisible coach." He thought that, like a parent, his job was to help his athletes become "responsibly independent," to allow them to develop a sense of ownership in their own training, their own advancement, and their own team. I know that the best teams that I ever coached effectively learned to coach themselves. They drove each other to their combined success with their enthusiasm, their mutual support, and the guidance and experience of their older teammates. As my coaching experience grew, I learned to "pull away" from coaching such groups to allow the team's internal coaches to lead. Any such coaching is much more influential when the guidance comes from *within* the team.

Cross country and track & field are team sports, though the actual athletic performance is mostly an individual effort. But, anybody who thinks they stand alone needs to have their head examined. When we are fortunate enough to win a trophy at the national championships, we take a team photo. But in that photo, we don't just include the top seven runners and the coaches. We make sure to include any team member who has been able to attend the meet. It is the collective spirit of our entire team that makes our winning possible, and they all share in the honor of our good or great performances.

I should say more emphatically that it is the work of our entire team *and our entire coaching staff* that has made our winning possible. For almost 40 years, Frank Gramarosso—Grammy—has been my assistant coach in cross country and track & field. It's very clear to me that our program wouldn't have had the success we've had—I wouldn't have been able to be as successful a coach—without Frank's constant help and support. More specifically, we *never* had great success in track & field until Frank joined me in coaching at North Central. The year we won our first cross country title, we scored only 2 points in the NCAA national track meet the following spring. This was before Frank arrived.

We've won 12 track & field titles (outdoors and indoors) since Frank began coaching with me, and our program has been at its best since Frank took over the head coaching role 10 years ago. I'm very happy to report that Grammy has taken over from me as head cross country coach beginning with our 2020 season as well, and our team and alumni are delighted that he is going to lead our teams and carry our traditions forward into the future. Words can barely express how thankful I am to have had Frank, and dozens of volunteer coaches, at NCC with me on this long journey with my teams.

Behind the Stripes

Why has North Central College Cross Country been so dominant for more than 50 years? What is the secret behind all the successful runners who come out of this program? What makes these candy stripes so special and... *magical*?

It is amazing how many times questions like these have been asked of Al, Grammy, alumni, and present athletes at North Central. The answers are quite simple, but they are nearly impossible to explain to those not directly involved. For the answers lie in the attitudes, passions, support, commitment, dedication, and tradition that are part of the souls of many present North Central runners, past North Central runners, Grammy, and Al. All of these things revolve around a *lifestyle* that we are devoted to religiously. As a direct result, these runners experience the unexplainable "feeling" that cannot be matched through anything else—and will never be forgotten.

Attitude and Passion are very important to a successful North Central runner. These are the motivating factors behind all the hard work. The true North Central runner does not run for any materialistic awards, titles, or praises that come from success. Likewise, even though he loves to run and finds it enjoyable, this is not the complete reason either. Also, there is no mythical "runner's high" that possesses a runner during the sixth hill at Blackwell Forest Preserve or the last repeat mile at Lincoln Park. Finally, running has its own health benefits too, but this again is not the reason.

A North Central runner runs because of his attitude and passion for what lies behind the sport. He runs for the personal satisfaction of pushing his body to its extreme limitations. He wants to suck out every bit of potential his body possesses, constantly asking himself, "How far can I go?" He not only wants to be the best, and conquer anyone or anything that stands in his way. More importantly, he wants to conquer himself. He's always pushing, thinking, and engaging on ways of doing this. Something always in the back of his mind is that there is more in his body than he has shown—and he works to pry it out, sacrificing every ounce of energy to do so. There is no stopping him. He is focused on the "task" and will not let anything distract him from completing it.

Why does he do this?

To be faster by a tenth of a second, by an inch, by two feet or two yards than he had been the week or year before… to conquer the physical limitations placed upon him by a three-dimensional world. If he could conquer the weakness, the cowardice in himself, he would not worry about the rest; it would come. Training was a rite of purification; from it came speed, strength; racing was a rite of death; from it came knowledge. Such rites demand,

if they are to be meaningful at all, a certain amount
of time precisely on the Red Line where you can
lean over the manicured putting green at the edge
of the precipice and see exactly nothing.

—*John L. Parker, Once a Runner*

This pursuit for excellence is something that cannot be
matched by any other sport. It is an internal feeling, passion, and attitude that exists. Those who possess it, know
it. Those who don't will never know.

Runners with this type of attitude make up North Central's team, and this is where the next important ingredient
comes in—Support. One of the reasons for our success is
that the atmosphere surrounding everyone on the team is
an interconnecting network of love, commitment, and support for one another. The cross team is not a social club, just
here to hang out and have a good time together. We have a
greater purpose. It is a group of guys who would give their
lives to help each other through anything, because they
know the others would do the same for them. We are a team
and a family. We go through the good times together and
hell together to get there. The purpose: to push each other
to become the best runners and people we are capable of
becoming, and beyond. There is a constant "building up"
process. There are no *teardowns*. There is no *negativity*.
These are left to the cowards. We feed off of each other's
positive attitudes and successes.

Teammates like these are the ones who you can look
at and be completely honored to be associated with. These
are the guys who will always leave everything they have on
the course for their team, no matter where they finish in a
meet. These are also the guys who can go to bed every night

and honestly say to themselves, "I did everything I could do today to make myself the best possible runner I could be." It is such a powerful feeling to line up at the starting line with these guys, look to the right and to the left, and know all of this before the race begins.

This support system is something other teams have tried to emulate and sometimes failed. But they fail if the chanting, words, and hoopla are not sincere. What we have is very real—you can literally feel the support chilling at your bones, but giving warmth to your blood during a Monday or Wednesday workout. It is felt no matter how far your teammates are away, and it will stay with you beyond college. It is absolutely true that, "Actions and feelings speak louder than words."

The next important ingredient is the dedication and Commitment for which everything is carried out. Cross country may be the most physically demanding sport there is because the athlete is constantly working on taking his body and mind to their complete culmination. There are no shortcuts in running. The only way to improve time after time is to simply run day after day, month after month, and year after year, with the proper balance of quality and recovery runs. The two-hour runs are the heart and foundation that mold the body into a toned, hard, unbreakable tank. The ten-to-fifteen-mile tempo runs are the fuel—for without them, you will never grow as a distance runner. These are runs that you must dig down deep to find out what you are made of when you feel like you can't go further. [See "One Winter Monday" below.] But you push through and it makes the body and the mind so tough that they cannot be broken.

Now there will be times when you feel like you train your guts out for what seems like eternity and find little improvement. Everyone goes through this. It's called "The

Trials of Miles, the Miles of Trials." Don't get frustrated. It's consistency over a long period of time that makes you stronger and stronger. Once you finally break through, there is no turning back.

Finally, Tradition is the best constituent that adds to the environment that is so special at North Central. No other team in the United States has the powerful tradition that we do. Most of what you learn about the program you will learn from your upperclassmen. We call it the "Passing down of the torch." There is no such thing as a lowly freshman who does not matter to us until he is older and stronger. In fact, it's the exact opposite. We take very special interest in our freshmen. The upperclassmen, alumni, Grammy, and Al are here for you to learn from. The tradition lies in passing down information, feelings, commitment, and attitudes that we learned to those who are eager to learn. For one day, you will not only be a part of the team—you will be the heart of the team. Then it will be your responsibility to do the same thing.

Every year builds upon itself in this way. It started when Al started running—then went on to our founding fathers like Eric Thornton and Glenn Behnke—and it continued to be passed down and will continue to be throughout the decades at North Central. And every year, something new is learned or developed that is combined with the old, and passed down. This is how our program has evolved into what it is today.

Now, the point of this essay is not to tell you what you must do to be a success here. It is to give you a glimpse of what North Central is all about, so you can make a choice. We run in an atmosphere of freedom here to ensure that everyone does what he wants to, without any pressure. The successful distance runners here are that way because they chose to be. They chose to devote themselves to a certain lifestyle, 365 days a year, that is not easy. Those who are not successful here as runners are that way because they choose not to be. These are the ones who hardly run in the summer. They go through the motions, and are content with letting others put in the hard work—while they watch on the sidelines, pretending to have "lived the life" but knowing deep down they have not. They never earn the stripes.

There may only be seven runners that represent our team at nationals, but there are many more who deserve it. Those who live the life completely with no regrets, doing everything along the way they can for themselves and their teammates, whether they run nationals or not, are in the "top seven" as well. They may not be on the course physically, but mentally and spiritually they are there, running along with the other seven, helping them dig down deep for that extra strength. Without these guys, there would be no National Championship teams at North Central. So do you want to be a boy who goes through the motions and never earns his stripes? Or do you want to be a man who gives 100% to the team and to himself? It is completely your choice.

A combination of this attitude, passion, support, commitment, and tradition make North Central cross country the special thing it is today. There are no secrets to why we are so dominant and successful, and there are no words to describe why it is so special. But, something can be said of the *magic* of the stripes. They represent everything I have talked about. When you put on the stripes, you are putting on every race and practice that has ever been run at North Central. You are putting on every experience that has ever been learned at North Central. In fact, you are a part of every person that has ever been a part of this program. You will feel all of this when you put on those stripes. Now you can call it Tradition. You can call it Superstition. You can call it the way the material feels on you, and you may even call it a bunch of bull. But, I call it magic—and soon you will too.

—*John Weigel, Class of 1996*

One Winter Monday

The pace seemed to start off a little quicker than last time. Even before we hit the first stop sign, just behind the field house, the apprehension had started to creep into my soul slowly like a dense morning fog. I felt as if I was waiting in line for my first roller coaster ride. I was excited, but nervous and a little unsure. The cold, mid-winter wind whipped at my face and penetrated my light running gear, making me feel as it I were stranded in the middle of the barren tundra. There was a certain pleasure in feeling the cold, though. I looked at it as something else that would make me tougher; faster; stronger; maybe even invincible. Weather like this was what separated the boys from the men. I know only the true distance runners were toughing it out in this, and I welcomed the bitterness in a strange but understandable way.

The pace steadily quickened, and soon the three of us were gliding down the snow-patched streets in unison—not paying attention—but knowing exactly what we were doing and where we were going. My apprehensive feeling was soon gone, and our idle conversation was beginning to dwindle, being vanquished by the sound of controlled, but somewhat heavy, breathing. We made our way through the snow-covered trail, my least favorite part of the run. It always seemed to break our rhythm in a moderately annoying fashion. But in no time at all, we were back on the roads, just at the pace where we left off.

I looked over and took in the surroundings for the first time. I'd run this route so many times, and it astonished me to realize how little I really recognized about it. The wooded area to the left looked naked at this time of year, only clothed by the freshly fallen snow that clung to the branches like cotton candy swirled around a stick. The snow looked so content and unbothered here. We ran on the shoulder of the busy road. The cars would not budge an inch and some even seemed to swerve at us. At times I could almost see the murderous grimace of a car taking on the personality of the driver, just to let us know that we did not belong on their road with them.

Finally, we turned onto the next side street, and it was then when I realized the run had really only just begun. Without speaking, the three of us picked up the already intense pace a few notches to a speed that most would think unbearable. This unspoken surge, that would only quicken as the run progressed, was something we neither envied nor resented. It was just another thing we did that we knew we had to do and didn't think twice about.

As we headed down the slight, curving hill, we ran by some people out on their sidewalks and driveways, staring at us with blank faces, just holding their shovels like time had frozen with the weather. I could not tell if they were in awe at the speeds we were running, or just stunned by the fact that we were out in weather that they thought of as something only attempted out of necessity with a snow shovel or ice scraper. Either way, they had absolutely no idea. I always feel a sort of pride, though, in those situations when "civilians" look upon us and think only words like "crazy" or "different." If they only knew that running, to me, was like food or sleep. It was something that I needed to survive, and I knew my companions felt the exact same way.

The next two to three miles seemed to go pretty quickly. I was now starting to fatigue, but not in a serious way. Running by "Green Valley" made me remember an incident last year on the same route. The words were still so clear. I remember our former captain, Derron Bishop, looking over at an agonizing Kyle Kirchhoff with a tormenting smile, saying, "Hey Kyle, we're 45 minutes into our run, and we're still running away from school!" He then gave a loud, cruel laugh. We all had a good laugh at the sinister, but good-humored prank. This same run, however, which was more of a moderate to steady run last year, had developed into a punishing tempo run this year that was in no way funny.

The pinnacle of our run was almost upon us. As we hit "Trillium" there was a short moment of triumph, although I knew it wouldn't last. We were a good seven miles into our run, nearly half-way, but the fact that we made it to this street—a street that had a diminutive mystique to it, in name only—was a heartwarming experience, even if only for a few seconds. And the run went on...

The next few miles were a blur. I made it through them, but I do not really remember much from them. I only had the feeling of continual strain on my cardiovascular system to remind me.

We ran by a group of kids playing in the snow. One asked us if we were running a marathon. Another chucked a snowball at us. We did not pay much attention to them at this point in the run. If one of us gave a chuckle or smile, I did not notice. And the run went on...

There was now complete silence. I could only hear the pounding of our feet and the heavy rhythmical breathing, only sometimes interrupted by an infrequent "farmer's blow" or short hack of the throat. As we ran along "Coach," the most agonizing, grueling street in Naperville, which seemed to last a lifetime, I was starting to get the usual doubt of whether I'd make it back alive. There was such a burning sensation in my lungs that I knew would not go away for a while yet. I felt like I could not get my legs moving fast enough and at any moment they would tie up. I wondered if my companions were in as much pain as I was. They looked like they were moving so effortlessly. I tried to disguise my struggle, but I just did not feel as smooth as they looked. I could not even feel the cold anymore. As a matter of fact, it was the furthest thing from my mind. The doubt crossed me again whether I'd make it back or not. I wondered how tough I really was. I knew, deep down though, that I wouldn't quit. I couldn't—not at this point. I was nearly four miles from home—a mere step compared to the amount of mileage we put in on a weekly basis. I was too close, and I knew my teammates would pull me through.

We worked so well together, the three of us. We knew each other almost as well as we knew ourselves on the road. We helped each other, yet pushed each other to perfection. I thought to myself how I could never let them down—or any of my teammates for that matter—because I knew they would never let me down. I would do anything for them because I knew they would do the same for me. If I fell off now, I would feel the guilt and shameful feeling of being broken, and it wouldn't go away until I redeemed myself. I then thought of all the goals I had for myself. How bad did I want them? I also thought of all the future races I would run when the inevitable point comes when you either let up or your break through. So, I formed a grimace on my face and decided there was no way in hell I was letting up. Instead of letting the feeling break me, I broke it. I left the pain behind, bellowing in the cold, lonely winter street, with no remorse.

We now headed up "heart-break hill" and I pushed it as hard as I could. "You ain't so bad!! You ain't nothin'!!" I thought to myself. I was talking to the hill. For me the run was over at this point. Now that I had broken through, the last two or three miles were nothing. I had run these streets so many times, I feel I could run them in my sleep. I did not even have to think. My legs would just carry me through. And the run went on…

As we headed into the final straight behind the field house, we were gleaming from the long journey we had just successfully completed. We slapped hands and smiled at each other with respect and approval at a run that seemed like it could not have gone any better. We were exhausted, but we were happy. It wasn't a happiness from being finished, but a happiness from pushing our bodies to their limits; a happiness derived from doing everything we could on that day to make ourselves the best possible runners we could be. I had never felt more satisfied with myself than at that point, and the only thing I could think to myself was, "Man, I can't wait 'till Wednesday."

—*John Weigel, Class of 1996*

Senior Day at the Park

It was the last park workout at Lincoln Park, Senior Day. The seniors were all out there for their final of many memorable gut-wrenching workouts. It started off as a normal Monday workout. The warm up, no different, and the spirits—well, a little apprehensive for what was to come.

The usual small talk was made as we stretched and changed shoes on the driveway. The weather was crisp and cool, like a usual late autumn day. The seniors, all a little less talkative than usual; trying to recapture as many moments as they could, but realizing no one workout really stood out. To tell the truth, I felt a little depressed. I always do on Senior Day because I can look at them and tell what they're thinking. They want it to last forever, but they know it has to end sometime.

Well, the time came when the workout was really about to begin. "All set?" I said. "You bet," the group replied in unison. We were off...

The first part of the 800 was no different, the pace about the same along with the feeling. We rounded the first corner, taking turns to make sure we didn't run each other into a tree. We filed along the edge of the river in a line, making sure to jump the eroded part of the trail. As we grouped up and stepped the ditch, we headed toward the final straight-away. I was already starting to get a little tired.

But just as I started to really concentrate, I heard a huge roar from ahead. Lined up along the finish area were a group of guys yelling and screaming at us to get through that 800. The air was filled with the enthusiasm of a group of runners more excited than I had ever seen them. They did the "wave" as we ran by, roaring, clapping, and slapping hands as we went. I had never heard such emotions and enthusiasm in a Monday workout. It was incredible.

The rest of the workout went by in the same fashion, but the enthusiasm spread to the entire team. The atmosphere couldn't be put into words, only lodged in the memories of those who were present. The depressing, monotonous feelings were now forgotten. Everyone became alive and joyful. We slapped hands, hugged, and jumped around like we had just won the national championships.

So, instead of the seniors leaving the park with memories that all ran together, depressed that it was their last Monday workout, they were given this gift. Ironically, it was the freshmen who gave it to them. I don't know what it is like to be a senior on "Senior Day" yet, but I do know one thing for sure: Those seniors will never forget that day. It will always stand out in their hearts and minds.

This experience shows that every single person on this team can contribute. Every person has something to give to help better us as a team. You don't have to be in the top seven to do that.

At that workout, I realized the freshmen knew what our program was all about. They captured the entire atmosphere of a great team, by bringing out the best in everyone. The freshmen reminded me that the whole process is supposed to be fun, especially for those that put in all the work along the way. We work for weeks, months, and even years to become the best we can become as runners. When we get to that point in the season when we are at our best, we have to be excited. Most other teams are tailing off. We are just getting the ball rolling.

I can already tell this is going to be a very special year. About everyone I've talked to is doing everything they can to be their best. That is what it takes. When we put all of these guys together, there is no telling what we can accomplish AS A TEAM."

—John Weigel, Class of 1996

John Weigel in these stories gives, I think, the view of our program from *within* the team that I could never provide as a coach from *above* the team, if you will. This is why I treasure the stories so, and felt they should be a part of this book. I believe, I hope, they show that many of our athletes, like John, "get it." They experienced our running program, understood and accepted our culture and its importance, saw its value, and worked to pass it on to the next generation of our runners. This is the attitude that we had long fostered early in our program—the attitude that I believe we lost for a while in the early 2000s—and what I believe we have rebuilt within our team in the many years since I first began writing this book.

Personally, I believe team feeling, of the kind John Weigel describes in these stories, is synonymous with love— and not the fleeting love of infatuation. Great teams are individuals bound together with a strong purpose, a shared common goal, and a collective realization that to be successful, they need one another. This is reflected by a trust in the commitment of living, intrinsically, with positive values for one another, rather than complying with a long list of detailed rules. These positive values include a commitment to personal growth, accountability for responsible behavior, and most important, selflessness.

This positive team value of selflessness can be seen clearly through a series of incredible episodes beginning in the spring of 1993 that involved several of our best runners at the time, and John himself. John Weigel, then a freshman at North Central, was competing in the 5,000-meter run, at our home track, in the College Conference of Illinois and Wisconsin (CCIW) Conference Track Championships. Also in the race were Dan Mayer, a junior, and Derron Bishop, a senior. After the first lap, these teammates joined together and, at the two-mile mark, all three broke away from the pack. After a time, Weigel, the youngest, began to struggle, but Bishop and Mayer stayed near him, helping him along, running just fast enough so that John could stay behind them and draft off them, but the pack could not catch up. In the final lap, Bishop and Mayer said, "John, you come up and win."

And that's exactly what happened. As a freshman, John Weigel became the 5,000-meter conference champion. Both Mayer and Bishop could have easily won the race, but chose to mentor Weigel and give the freshman the victory. They were clearly and incredibly unselfish. More than personal victory, they wanted to encourage this young teammate, for whom they had great respect. They wanted him to have that experience, that exhilaration, and essentially "passed the baton" of team feeling to the new generation.

The 1993 NCAA Cross Country Championships were held in Grinnell, Iowa, the following fall. At one point in the race, Weigel, now a sophomore, was running about 200 yards behind the leader, North Central senior Dan Mayer. Before long, Weigel had caught up to Mayer with relative ease. As the finish line drew near, Mayer—not knowing who was running so close behind him—turned and glanced over his shoulder. Weigel, returning the previous year's gift, said, "Don't worry. It's me. You're going to win." On that particular day, Weigel could have been the NCAA Division III National Champion—an opportunity that might never come again. Instead, he unselfishly honored his mentor with the national championship.

And this goes on. On that same team in 1993 was a freshman, Matt Brill. Brill came in 25th in those same national championships in Iowa. Throughout that season, John Weigel had been nurturing Brill, helping him to mature as a runner. And Brill observed Weigel's unselfishness at the end of that race.

Two years later, North Central was participating at the 1995 NCAA National Championships in La Crosse, Wisconsin. Brill, leading Weigel through most of the race, relinquished the lead near the end, refusing to pass his teammate into the finish. He could have won, but he wouldn't do it, having tremendous respect for Weigel. He wouldn't take the championship away from Weigel in his final race. It was beautiful. At the national meet the previous year, Weigel had finished second to a runner from Williams University.

Bridget Belgrovine, the Athletic Director at the University of Wisconsin—LaCrosse, witnessed this 1995 race in which Brill had chosen to accept second place. Soon after, she wrote the following letter to the North Central College Athletic Director:

The performance of two student athletes, John Weigel and Matt Brill, were particularly impressive and warrant special note. While they finished 1-2, it was the way the race ended which will stand out in my mind as one of the greatest finishes I have witnessed in sports. Both young men remained close and methodically stretched their lead on the rest of the field while running the last two miles virtually alone. It was evident that a North Central College runner would win the 1995 national event.

What unfolded, however, was a true example of unselfish team spirit exhibited by a young man that deserves recognition. As the two runners approached the last 100 meters, Matt Brill was witnessed urging his teammate John Weigel to go ahead… to cross the line and win it. Either runner could have easily sprinted ahead but Matt made the decision to let his teammate, a senior, finish first, and for that I applaud his spirit of sportsmanship.

As I handed Matt his All-American certificate, I could not help but believe that on this day he had the opportunity to be the National Champion in that cross country race. However, he passed it up to a senior teammate, who I learned had finished second the previous two years. For his performance, Matt is truly a National Champion in the sport of life.

But this story doesn't really end, even here after that wonderful tribute. By Matt Brill's senior year, he had not been a national champion—he had not even been a conference champion. In fact, despite his promising freshman year, Brill had not won a single cross country race in three years. The one race he could have won, at nationals in 1995, he had chosen not to, in consideration of his teammate. But sometimes, you win in losing, especially when you are part of and supported by a great group of teammates. Matt Brill won only one race in four years at North Central—the Division III National Cross Country Championship his senior year. What a reward for a wonderful teammate!

Matt, like Weigel and Meyer and Bishop before him, provided support and set a great example for his teammates for four years, and their examples have inspired our team every year since. They showed that running together reduces individual fear and improves individual (and group) performances. I repeat, "Great teams are individuals bound together with a strong purpose, a shared common goal, and a collective realization that to be successful, they need one another." This type of team selflessness, this type of mentoring and support, this type of Personal Best, this type of tradition, is what makes North Central College's men's cross country and track & field athletes true champions.

"Team! Team! Team!"

CHAPTER 9

Culture

"I'm one. All I need is four more guys."
—Derron Bishop

"The spiritual components of the athletic experience are at least as important, and provide the solid foundation upon which to build and sustain the physiological improvements."
—Coach Al Carius

"The three most important words relating to the long-term success of a program are culture, culture, and culture."
—Coach Al Carius

I will admit that even after over 50 years of coaching, I am still not a great recruiter. I really enjoy talking to a prospective recruit, and his parents, who has an interest in running at North Central. But, going out, "beating the bushes," and trying to find the guys who fall between the cracks of academically rigorous schools or less expensive public schools like state universities has never been my strength. I'm excited if a student has a sincere interest in

North Central College because he feels it is the best fit for him. And I appreciate and enjoy the dialogue, with the student and his parents, related to the student having found the best place for himself academically, socially, and athletically. My sensitivity on this subject goes back to my own college search, as I discussed previously. But I loved talking to any prospective athlete or student who envisioned the North Central experience adding future value to their lives.

In the early years of the program, I didn't really have to recruit. I didn't recruit Glenn Behnke, who in 1974 became our first NCAA National Champion in track & field. I didn't recruit Jeff Milliman, who would go on to become North Central's first individual national champion in cross country in 1980. I didn't even know who Jeff was when he arrived on campus. As it turns out, he was a state champion in Florida. To this day I'm still not sure how he even heard of North Central College. In my early years, for the most part, I primarily talked to student-athletes who had selected North Central on their own. And our track & field program absorbed off-season athletes from other programs like football.

Regardless of how they found their way to North Central, I'm glad they did! Guys like Glenn and Jeff, Scott Barrett and Jim and Jon Macnider, Dave Hartmann and Steve Jawor, John Weigel, Nick Hird, Julius White, Mike Spain, Gary Peterson, Johnny Crain, Adam Pennington, Matt Osmulski, Jims Dickerson, Kurt Hasenstein, Dennis Piron, Brian Johnson, Jeff Stiles, Bob Dunphey, Wendel McCraven, Dru Patel, and Dan Meyer, just to name a few. They showed me early on the importance of having strong internal leadership on a team—a critically important internal nucleus for a program's cultural foundation. "A leader is one who knows the way, goes the way, and shows the way," according to John C. Maxwell. I learned that these are the type of athletes who lead by example while I, the coach, am not around. And leadership coming from a peer within the team is far more influential than that which comes from a coach.

Derron Bishop was another example of a natural internal leader. He came in at the right time, when our program really needed a respected new leader. Most of the previous year's varsity team had graduated when he arrived as a freshman in the fall of 1989. But Derron wasn't daunted, even as a freshman. Our young team was meeting together, wondering who might become our new top group, the leaders to replace the great runners who had graduated the previous year. Looking around the room, Derron stepped forward and said, "I'm one. All I need is four more guys."

Derron's words reminded his teammates that each year it's a new team, and the positions of "team leaders" and "top five" are available for any runner to work to secure. He made it clear that you were either with him or you weren't. He was someone our team rallied around. He was one, and he inspired others to try and work to be one of the other four runners needed to score in a cross country meet. Obviously, there were more than five guys on the team. But with Derron's leadership, work ethic, and inspiration, they *all* got better over time by following his lead. What we become is very strongly influenced by who we surround ourselves with.

A positive atmosphere is critically important for a team, and what you're surrounded by has a measurable impact on your outcome. This is true not just in running, but in academics, in your career, and in many other aspects of your life. I recall a time when I was talking to a highly successful football coach about the importance of the environment on a team. At the time, this coach was having difficulty with his team's culture. There were divisions within his team, almost as if he and some of the players were reading from different playbooks. He told me, "Al, it's tough enough going into battle with the bullets coming at your face. But it's far worse when the bullets are coming at your back."

What you must pay attention to in order to maintain a team's positive atmosphere can be as simple (and yet as profound) as the body language of individual team members. The atmosphere surrounding your team is deep and influential. Geno Auriemma, legendary women's basketball coach at the University of Connecticut, stated: "I am always checking out for what's going on on the bench. If somebody's asleep over there, if somebody doesn't care, if somebody's not engaged in the game, they will never *get* in the game."

At the beginning of this book, I made reference to the slow erosion of our culture within our program which, I believe, led to our 12th place finish at the 2005 national championships. The outcome of that race helped me redirect and focus my attention on the numerous breaks in the continuity and stability of our culture which had crept within our program. Any team can have a bad race—start out too fast on a hilly course or too slow on a tight, narrow course. But I had sensed a problem developing more regularly within our team and had not figured out, even as an experienced coach, how to address it. That poor finish was an alarm bell ringing, with blessings hidden within our difficulties.

Leading up to that season, I thought we had a well-established set of foundational values we shared with our team that seemed to me were passed on like a baton from one class to the next. I felt like we were on autopilot and cruise control for sustained, lasting success. We'd bring in new freshmen and they'd learn from the upperclassmen, and the important history of traditions and work ethics would be passed on naturally from one team to the next. For a long time, too long, I was content to let it be. I was coaching in the dark. In part, I assumed "Why mess with success?" But somewhere along the way, I overlooked something as a coach, and missed the weakening changes that were occurring on my team, undermining our foundation. I was distracted, or oblivious, and complacent, by enjoying the external accolades that came with our long string of successes.

I have a clearer view now of what I missed as a coach, from the other side of the abyss. It sounds so serious to say it that way, but if I'm going to tell you our story and the lessons I've learned, I must tell you the truth. Over 32 seasons, from the beginning of NCAA Division III in 1973 until 2004, our North Central cross country team finished out of the top four in the nation only once. Our 12 titles were accompanied by 12 second-place finishes, and five times we were third. Our lowest place before 2005 was seventh. Clearly we were doing something right as a program, consistently, for many years. So our first really poor national finish in 2005 was a shock to me. I did a lot of soul searching, then and since, to determine the mistakes I made and how I could improve as a coach to bring our program back. I hoped to progress by transforming our weaknesses into future strengths.

But, what had to be changed and reformed from this point on to bring back the success that has followed? Well, it had to begin with my taking complete responsibility for the most important element of a team—the culture.

What I re-learned was this. A team is like a garden where you're planting the seeds for success. Our athletes are the seeds, who *want to grow*, who come to college wanting to run and to work to become their best selves. You invite them to grow in the soil of your program. But, you have to provide rich earth and furnish everything your garden, your seeds need to thrive—water, fertilizer, and sunlight. Some of the seeds require more sunlight, some more water. Some seeds climb naturally toward the sun, some need to be trained up a trellis, or provided with more support to fully prosper. A gardener can't expect good results by just scratching the seeds into the ground, forget about weeding, and walk away.

Neither can a coach. That's coaching on autopilot. I had a responsibility to my athletes to teach them actively, to tend them, to guide them, to "train them up in the way they should grow." I was mistaken to believe that a team's culture is adopted naturally, almost automatically by new athletes. Instead it must be tended to constantly, and reinforced repeatedly—like teaching good manners and proper English to young children.

I now believe that the three most important words relating to the long-term success of an athletic program are culture, culture, and culture—but it must be the *right* culture. Great workouts, teamwork, positive leadership, and an appropriate *culture* contribute to a successful team. I as a coach was responsible for nurturing all these factors for my teams—for tending my garden, for focusing my attention on team culture, for leading better when my team needed more inspiration and direction.

While I attended the University of Illinois, I was fortunate to hear the inspirational coach, Ray Elliot, speak on numerous occasions. His speeches were electric with passion, and at least one of them is available to listen to today via a recording of a vinyl record on YouTube. While at North Central, I once saw a visiting coach trying to motivate his team by sitting them around a record player and playing one of Coach Elliot's speeches! I believe the direct communication of an important message to a team is the responsibility of the head coach, and cannot be delegated to someone else. The coach must be the central authentic messenger.

Here's another big mistake I know I made, one which was very difficult for me to recognize, and then to comprehend. As a gardener at home, I should have known better. My misconception was that if athletes joined the team, I *assumed* they loved to run and had a hunger for getting better. I didn't understand that there could be weeds growing in our garden. There could be individuals who were on the team for the wrong reasons. Some were there merely for the social aspect of being part of a team, which is understandable. From a psychological perspective, we all have the inherent desire to feel included. Others merely wanted the prestige of identification by saying they ran for North Central College.

Whatever the reason for their actions, I slowly realized these team members weren't focused on their being coached for self-improvement. They therefore were not adding to the team in a positive way by striving for their best, and working for the best for the team. I thought back again to the wisdom of Coach Geno Auriemma from Connecticut, who noted, "Bad body language [among your athletes] matters because it poisons the team. It's a distraction. It affects performance throughout the lineup... It's a reaction [by one or more athletes] to an event that, if perceived negatively by a teammate, instantly starts to unravel the thread of the team."

I heard once that over 80% of what we are surrounded by on a daily basis is negative. Therefore, it is imperative that the practice environment and atmosphere our athletes enter each day counters that negativity with firmer, fertile, positive ground. The coach must keep the soil rich, the garden healthy, and cleared of weeds.

When I ran, it was because I wanted to do it. I hated the feeling I had at the University of Kansas where it became a job and a business. It sucked the fun out of running, to the point where I didn't even know if I wanted to do it anymore. It was the wrong environment for me to grow. I found the right culture at the University of Illinois.

Coming to North Central was an opportunity for me to recreate a new culture, and I mistakenly assumed that everyone on our team year after year just naturally loved to run as I did, and had a passion to get better. Otherwise, why would they be here? Each year, and for many years, our garden grew and bloomed. But with time, there were more and more weeds—because I was complacent and ignored the soil's richness.

I had always used the morning run as a sort of thermometer for the emotional health of the team. Every morning at 6:30 a.m., the team gathers behind the Merner Fieldhouse and goes on an easy four-mile run. This run was always optional, and actually a sociable team-building exercise. I didn't want to *make* people run. Not in the morning, not ever! You were there because you wanted to be there, intrinsically—it was an opportunity to get better. I saw through the years, however, that our numbers on the morning run were slowly dwindling. On one occasion, I had a runner who asked me to run across campus each morning to go to his second-floor room *to wake him up each morning!* I soon realized this was a big mistake. Two of the main benefits of our morning run were the self-discipline and the reinforced confidence that accumulated daily from the athlete making the decision personally to get up and run in the morning.

On the Tuesday morning of the National Championships week in the fall of 2005, there were only two of our top seven athletes on the morning run. Afterward, I told Ray Krauss, an alum who served as one of our volunteer assistant coaches, "We're in trouble."

Gradually, our culture and our collective lifestyle were becoming weaker, and I hadn't seen the warning signs. We had shirked our work ethic, our passion, our cohesiveness as a team. We had lost what made the 1975 No Names team elevate one another despite their lack of individual gifted talents. There was a sense of complacency that grew from our history of repeated success. It appears, in retrospect, that many of our runners came to believe that success at season's end—more top-three finishes—would come automatically without doing the necessary work throughout (and before) the season. *"We're North Central! Wait until the end of the year, we'll put on the stripes. We'll be there."* The 2005 season was a wake-up slap in the face to me because, talent-wise, I knew we were a far better team than 12th in the nation. "Winning takes talent," Coach John Wooden noted. "To repeat takes character." I needed to refocus us on character.

Although I am not a fan of anonymous postings on the

internet, there are a couple of them from '05 and '06 that I keep in a drawer of my desk. I look at them every now and again as inspirational messages to me. They give feedback and a perception of our North Central performance, and culture, from the outside:

> *"North Central is terrible and will remain that way for a while. They might do ok in cross but c'mon what have they even done in track recently? Two years ago, they sucked… this past year they were terrible… oh wait, [one of their runners] did get last in the 10k, watch out!!!"*

And another, posted right after our 12th place finish:

> *"Well, as some of you guys may know, this is the first time that North Central College has finished out of the top 3 in over 25 years. I predict a changing of the guard. Big Al has been coaching for 35 years now, so he is probably on his way out with NCC losing all of their top athletes next year. Calvin is returning everyone next year except for their 4 and their young guns will be experienced next year and the following year to keep their program on top.*
>
> *Let's take a moment of silence as the nation's top program will falter for at least a decade… Al Carius, thank you and it has been a pleasure."*

I gotta tell you, those comments were tough to take. But, as Dr. Phil once said, "You can't change what you don't acknowledge." Then I again I thought about Waubonsie

Valley High School counselor Jim Braun and how he told me that some kids today often lack the intrinsic desire and tools to navigate from where they are today to achieving their goals. There is a relationship between his words and what I realized in 2005. Something was missing within our program, below the depth of our training and workouts.

A very wise woman once shared a moment of enlightenment with me when she stated, "Privilege is a learning disability." At times, we are all so busy working toward material outcomes for our youths that we don't have time for the most important values within character that they require to succeed. I had to again find the steps leading to our goal and retake each one. This renewal of our program had to begin with me. I had to take a close look within myself and consider what it was I was communicating to my team.

Another friend from Waubonsie Valley came to visit me in my office some years ago. Kevin Rafferty is an alum of our program who serves as Waubonsie Valley's cross country and track & field coach. As we talked, the topic of "helicopter parents" came up, with their well-intentioned intervening in the lives of their children at the first sign of stumbling along the path of life. Kevin informed me that he has seen this expanded to what he called "snowplow parents," who plow ahead of their children to "clear the path" of potential obstacles and adversity.

The problem is that this natural parental protectiveness inhibits some advantages to children of working toward self-realization and potential growth that comes when facing inevitable normal daily life challenges. Oddly enough, sometimes we want to help our children—and athletes—succeed so much that we end up causing them to bypass experiences that stimulate important internal wisdom and development.

My son Brent shared with me another insightful piece of advice that he heard from a speaker at a teachers' institute. In summary, the speaker inferred that today's standard education is at times draining the humanity out of the students' maturation process, and interfering with their development of their own intrinsic motivation. This happens when schools over-emphasize the *outcome* of standardized tests instead of reinforcing the aspects of learning that inspire the student's *process* of education. We should, as ever, listen to Socrates, who counseled, "Education is the kindling of a flame, not the filling of a vessel."

Now, what does this have to do with running and sport? I have always felt that though the workout is the physiological basis for sustaining speed from, say 40 meters on to any distance, the *spiritual* components of the athletic experience are even more important, and provide the solid foundation upon which to build and sustain the athlete's physiological and psychological improvements. This concept was reinforced by Dr. Jeff Duke.

After the 2005 national championship race, I met with assistant coach Frank Gramarosso and internal student leaders Julius White and Nick Hird, who would go on to be appointed our team captains the following season. They all told me the same thing: "You need to start requiring the morning run and demanding greater accountability within our training system."

I pushed back against the idea—the thought of *making* people run ran counter to my whole coaching philosophy! But Nick Hird gave the best defense of the idea. He said, "Al, if you require the morning run, it's not going to bother the guys who are intrinsically motivated. They're going to be there anyway. It's going to expose those guys who aren't, who have not bought into the philosophy and don't want to do it."

Those words made me realize I had to cultivate my garden. How could I relate with guys who didn't have the internal servo-mechanism—the intrinsic desire to run and get better? I had to go back to our philosophy, back to the basics. Run for Fun and Personal Bests. Run for Fun and *Personal* Bests! I don't care how fast or slow you are. But if you're not striving to get better, you're not living the philosophy.

I was reminded by Grammy and these two great team leaders that to be an effective leader, a better coach, sometimes your decisions will not be popular with everyone. But, you must consistently make decisive choices based upon what you intuitively feel to be in the best interests of the individual and the team. Over the years, I've come to recognize that one's intuition is a very important part of the process of choosing what is the best soil for your garden.

Still, I will admit, I was astonished at the backlash I received from some athletes on the team when I made the morning run mandatory. "We *have* to run?" Sadly a number of them ended up choosing to leave the program. Still, I had to tend my garden for the benefit of those who stayed.

I instituted a second change as well. I started standardizing more clear specifics within our workouts. For years I had told everyone, "Make the workout work for you." I said this with the expectation that runners were eager to improve and would read their bodies effectively to fine tune in order to get the maximum benefit from each training session. Some days an athlete is under the weather, and may need more recovery from an especially tough workout, and can intuitively tell his body needs more rest. But, increasingly, this internal program flexibility was taken by some athletes as an excuse to cut corners and repeatedly take the easiest path through challenging workouts. Some did not understand the core concepts of our training. Many did not really know themselves physically, mentally, emotionally, or spiritually, and thus weren't able to "make the workout work effectively" for themselves.

In yet another adjustment, I used to take every athlete to Blackwell Hill on Wednesdays. Our standard workout there is a five-mile building tempo, six hills, and a three-mile fartlek run back to the start. In recent years, however, we had more and more runners who would choose to do only three or four hills and then form an impromptu cheering section for the others who did all six. Now I'm sure if a runner is completing the full workout, it is nice to have people encouraging you as you're struggling up an enormous hill for the sixth time. But standing and cheering doesn't do anything for the guys standing on the sidelines. In fact, it detracts from those athletes running the full three parts of the training plan to see the growing number of teammates, and their body language, stopping short of our workout objectives.

From that point on, I had to create a rule: "You only go to Blackwell if you can complete the specific workout." It was effectively a minor coaching adjustment, but it had a big impact. One result was that, in some way, it became a *privilege* and an honor to be able to run our tough Black-well hill workout each week. As an athlete, you didn't get to go if you were injured or not ready to complete the entire training session. These were a few hard but key decisions for me as a coach, who had always run for the intrinsic love of the sport. But I remembered the words of the great

Coach John Wooden: "I treat everyone fairly, but I don't treat everyone equally."

Again, the professor I had at the University of Illinois, Dr. Glenn Blair, once said succinctly, "You reinforce the behavior that you want." So, another major adjustment that I made was that we started having short team meetings before and after every morning and every afternoon run to review the concept and objectives of that workout. I reminded myself of George Bernard Shaw's insight: "The single biggest problem in communication is the illusion that it has taken place." If I could no longer assume that our team culture was being passed on naturally, internally, among our athletes, I as a coach had to adjust, step up, and fill that void to make certain our culture of values and history were being explained from one generation to the next. These meetings were private and transparent. We could all speak freely, and I assured everyone that whatever was spoken stayed within the room.

At these meetings, I began to talk repeatedly about the behavior and values of character that I'm looking for that lead to success. I talk about the virtues and qualities within that make for greatness: intrinsic motivation, resilience, commitment, loyalty, discipline, positive expectations, being a team player. The workout might not be the same for everyone. But I wanted to reinforce for all my runners the internal strengths of Level-three character—the attitudes, concepts, and the many intangibles that foster wisdom in runners and teams, helping to create better citizens. I found too that I began to focus my time more on the guys who got it, who wanted it, those with the willingness and readiness to learn with the right attitude, and less time on those who didn't—or runners who tried to rely only on their natural talent.

I've spoken about the importance of internal leaders, and the freshmen class in the fall of 2006 was one of the best we ever had in that regard. Young men like Kyle Brady, Ryan Carrigan, and Sean Carlson would go on to become great runners. But even before that, they were natural leaders who bought into the culture and brought a level of positive energy to the team right when we needed it the most. Instead of thinking of themselves as freshmen, at the first opportunity they envisioned themselves as, and became, our varsity. And their positive perspective and confidence inspired and elevated the rest of our young team. We were "getting back to the basics," our solid foundational platform with the holistic integration of body, mind, and spirit.

Leadership, however, is not solely a natural, internal gift. A major element of effective leadership comes from the twists and turns of experience, and our young team had to learn their appropriate "competitive response" by trial and error. Although they were forming a stronger foundation, they did not yet have "the knowing," that deep, inner confidence and the positive expectations that results from the melding of mind, heart, body, and spirit. As I noted earlier, this lack of experience and confidence was demonstrated at the 2006 National Championship meet when our athletes were distracted by the mud and overall terrible conditions of the course and struggled to a 13th place finish. Calvin College, which had that collective "knowing" that we ourselves hoped to regain, won and dominated the race that year. Regardless of the conditions or any other external forces, Calvin's runners *knew* they were going to run well, and we were not yet at that level.

Again and again, I reassured the team that year that despite our 13th place finish, we were moving in the right direction. They listened with faith in the unseen. They were like sponges, absorbing everything I shared with them about the history and customs of past great teams and skillful leadership. I knew we were making the right changes and adjustments within the culture of the team. I knew that intuitively—though without concrete evidence—we were getting better. Unlike in 2005, we were connecting with our core values. We were coming together again and rebuilding a stronger framework. All I wanted for them was to finish higher than 12th place to show our young team, tangibly, that we were making progress. We did not receive tangible feedback for our intentional efforts, but we continued to move forward on faith in the unseen.

The 2007 Division III championship was at St. Olaf College in Northfield, Minnesota, and our next opportunity for appreciable positive feedback for our improving culture. Based on our regular season performances, I figured that if we ran well, we could finish as high as fourth. The previous week, at the regional championships, our North Central team started out too hard, not running the four parts of a balanced race, and ended up fading toward the end of the race.

We regrouped afterwards and agreed that at the national championship meet, they would be more conservative at the start. At this point, this coach knows now with hindsight, I should have been talking positively to my team about running the four parts of our own race once we got to nationals, instead of focusing on our mistake from the previous week. Our guidelines for running the four parts of a race are an absolute guide for our runners that is not undermined by external variables like bad running conditions. This should have been the message of my coaching strategy for them as we moved on to the national meet.

The next week, we were given a starting-line position in Northfield at the far left of the field of 30+ teams, and the course took a sharp right turn in the first 300 yards. It was a recipe for disaster. At the quarter-mile mark the runners took a wide right turn and North Central was still in dead last, with all the inside teams ahead of us. Our runners hit the narrowest part of the winding course and were just trapped on the narrow path. With nearly 300 competitors in the race, it was nearly impossible to make up ground. Kyle Brady was our top finisher that day, in 102nd place. The team finished 16th.

———

Once again, we did not receive the objective feedback I anticipated for what I knew were positive changes for the better within the culture of our team. I sensed we were getting better, but I was beginning to doubt myself as well. What if I *was* over the hill and didn't realize it? I knew there had to be doubt within the team as well, because the results were not matching what I was communicating in our daily meetings. Look at it from the perspective of those on the team: "Al says we're getting better and better, but the results don't bear that out. We made corrections after finishing 12th in 2005 and then got 13th in 2006. Now we're making more corrections and we keep hearing that we're doing things right, and then we get 16th!"

I worried I was losing my ability to evaluate where we were, and the team's trust in my credibility as well. It's like going into a class expecting to get an A and getting a D instead. How can you be off by that much and still be an effective, trustworthy coach? Was I rationalizing and making excuses for our performance and my leadership, or was this just reality?

After that race I gathered everyone together and said, "I don't care what anybody else from the outside says. I don't care. We're getting better on the inside! I want you to know I believe in you and that we are making progress, even if it doesn't look like it from the outside." I didn't want the team to think I had any doubt in them, or in myself. Certainly, they were exposed to enough uncertainty already, whether it was in their own minds or through anonymous posts on the internet saying that North Central's days as a national title contender were over.

The next fall of 2008, we brought back almost the entire varsity squad. Over the course of that season, I felt that our momentum was continuing to build and we were finally starting to put all the pieces together. With each race, our runners steadily improved, growing with confidence into a more cohesive and synergistic group. They were developing the knowing. I will admit, there was still a lingering doubt. After all, I was confident that we were getting better throughout the previous two seasons, but in each case the result at the national championship race was worse than the year before it. Everything pointed to the 2008 squad being a great team. Still, I felt stress like I never have before. I knew my runners must be feeling immense pressure as well.

That year, in Hanover, Indiana, our team proved to themselves what they were made of, and finished second nationally behind SUNY-Cortland. They were devastated that they didn't win, they had wanted a win so badly. But as a coach, I was unbelievably relieved and proud of them. Thank God, we got better! That team easily had more weight on their shoulders than any other team in the history of North Central's cross country program. They could just as easily have overreacted and bombed the race under the pressure of expectations. Had we fallen apart that year, that would have probably meant the end of North Central's program as we knew it. We would have lost all continuity with our history, and I would have lost all credibility as a coach.

That 2008 team saved our program. My worry was not that they didn't have the physical talent, not that they couldn't run well. My worry was that they were going to overreact with so much emotional stress on themselves that they would get too tense and try too hard for "outcome" at the expense of the four parts of the race, the "flow of process" within the race. I was so relieved that we returned to the podium that year and that we had finally received tangible, reinforcing evidence of our progress. That team showed me, and showed themselves, that these things I was preaching—messages on values, our culture, mileage, specific workouts—were starting to get traction, build momentum, and could continue to bring the desired results.

Those runners who were freshmen in 2006, who had endured one of the toughest stretches in our program's history, helped rebuild our program from its very foundation. The past four years they had heard the same encouraging messages from me and our other coaches, and collectively they listened, absorbed, and slowly returned to the proven formula and foundation of our success. They grew, built upon the best parts of their solid base: great character and the development of a deep intrinsic confidence in themselves and each other called "the knowing." They "knew" they would run well and be at their best in the season and the meets ahead.

The 2009 NCAA Division III National Championships in Cleveland were held on a very hilly and soft course. Despite the challenging conditions, North Central scored just 50 points and outdistanced second-place Williams College by 131 points. At the time it was the largest winning margin in NCAA Division III history. North Central was back, and our runners proved that they finally had the knowing.

The 12th, 13th, and 16th places at the national championships over the preceding years had felt like successive gut punches, each worse than the last. [This difficult period for our program is discussed plainly in a film documentary, "16-2-1 and Beyond: The Fall and Rise of North Central Men's Cross Country Team," by Alum R. J. McNichols.] Now North Central's runners finally had experienced a national championship again. We had concrete proof that we had gotten better from the inside out. For the seniors that year, the national title was the culmination of all their hard work, all the miles they had put in, the time spent together developing that team synergy and collective confidence. The seeds from 2006 were now in full bloom.

But, for me it was just the beginning. I'd seen what the weeds of complacency could do. Now that we had regained our cultural foundation, how could we sustain that year in and year out going forward? Since that 2008 season when North Central reclaimed a place on the podium, the team has finished first or second at the NCAA Division III National Championships nearly every year since. [2009-1st, 2010-2nd, 2011-1st, 2012-1st, 2013-2nd, 2014-1st, 2015-5th, 2016-1st, 2017-1st, 2018-1st, 2019-2nd, 2020—cancelled due to COVID-19] From the outside, it might seem like we are once again on autopilot, in a self-sustaining pattern of success.

But I had learned that success is not automatic. The right team culture is my number one responsibility, and in my opinion should be the number one focus of every coach. I'm much more in tune now to the spiritual character of everyone who joins the program. I no longer assume that they all have the right mindset, want to get better, or can contribute to our program via one of our three criteria. As I've discovered, it can be very easy for the weeds of complacency to creep in. My mistake was assuming that our program's positive culture was natural, not something that needed to be nurtured and cultivated. I will give everyone on the team the opportunity to adopt our team values, to run for fun and personal bests, to work on making the most of their God-given talent, until I can't do it effectively anymore. I treat everyone "fairly, but not equally." I must continually focus on tending my garden and keeping the soil rich.

When I recruit, which is still challenging for me at times, I look for the men with an intrinsic disposition of character who want to get a great education and love to run. They can be runners who might not be talented enough or run fast enough in high school to get the attention of a Division I program, or any collegiate program for that matter. But more important, if they show they have passion and a desire to run for fun and personal bests? These are the heart and soul runners, guys like Guthrie Hood, who was an inspiration to everyone because of who he was and the values he reflected. Everybody can bring that attitude, and if they do, then they're on this team.

I've had to learn and accept that not every athlete who comes to North Central will reflect such "winning" qualities. It still pains me to say our morning run is required, but it has to be a standard in order to help keep our culture pure, on a solid foundation. Yes, there is a physiological benefit for our athletes, but it is also psychological—and at its best, spiritual. Being on the morning runs with teammates will help distinguish those athletes who are committed, disciplined, and motivated to bettering themselves and contributing to the team from those who aren't. It's the same reason we now standardize our workouts, and focus our coaching on maintaining and passing our team culture from one generation to the next.

Our goal is to help our young people to be their best by making the most of their God-given talents as athletes, and to continue to thrive when they leave college and enter the world as responsible, independent grownups. This is the same cultural goal I learned from my family, my church, and my school as a young man, and now focus to pass on as a coach.

Our workouts are important, but our culture isn't in the workouts. It's reflected *in* the athletes. Or, if it's not, it's my job as a coach to sow the right attitude among them, support each of them, nurturing their pursuit of their goals, and help them to be their best. Team culture is something much more intangible than the science of the physical workouts but, by comparison, far more important to the lasting success of the individual and the team.

"Pa Pa Run!"

"In a world that's becoming more materialistic, more
professional, more outcome-oriented, we believe to the
contrary that the ultimate competition is you against you,
in the real 'Ah ha' moments in your life."

—Coach Al Carius

"Why has North Central been so successful?" It's a
question I get a lot, and believe it or not, I still don't
know the best way to answer it, at least not in any
sort of concise way. The truth is, there's no one big secret to
our success or the program's longevity. Our striped jerseys
are not magic. Despite the tradition and the importance we
place in them, they are just fabric. There is nothing magic in
Naperville's water that will make someone a great distance
runner. The answer is derived from all the little lessons that
you learn after 50 years of coaching, all the little intangible
elements that add up to Run for Fun and Personal Bests.

I've done my best to learn from those I consider mentors, gather the pieces of insightful information from people
I admire, and turn them into lessons in life that I can impart
to my athletes. It has been a trial and error approach in the
pursuit of one goal: bring "Run for Fun and Personal Bests"

from a philosophy to a fundamental reality. I've worked to get our athletes to make the most of their God-given talents. And I've shown them the way by celebrating the positive baby steps—the personal bests they can achieve each week, month, or season through discipline and hard work—that can carry them to their distant goals. Athletes come here and climb mountains of personal performance, but they do so one step at a time.

I want to refer back to one of my opening statements about my foundational philosophy: "Most of what I know about coaching I learned in Sunday School." This fundamental viewpoint was reinforced and objectified while listening to Dr. Jeff Duke speak of his three-dimensional coaching concept: Level One—Physical, Level Two—Mind and Body, Level Three—the holistic combination of Body, Mind, and Spirit.

The body physiology can be trained and developed through progressive overload. A coach needs to have at least a basic understanding of how the body functions and responds to exercise. You wouldn't want to go for surgery saying, "I hope this works," and learn that the doctor has never performed an operation before and received terrible grades in medical school. It's part of my job to understand what makes a person run, and I mean that literally and figuratively.

For mind and body, you need to know how to communicate and have the "emotional intelligence" to be able to relate to people to coach effectively. How do you help an athlete deal with disappointment? How do you help them handle success? How do you help them discover and nurture their passion for running? You can't put the desire to run and to get better into someone. If you're not intrinsically motivated, you're not going to get the benefits of the servo-mechanism that compels you to reach for personal bests. Without motivation, there is no learning, no drive, and no passion.

The mind can be conditioned with experience and time, while the spirit, character, provides the solid platform from which the body and mind can continue to grow and be sustained. This spirit—the values and virtues that make up character—is by far the most intangible element of coaching, but is critically important. Mind and body can't prosper without a spiritual foundation. How many times have you seen someone who can't reach or maintain their true potential because they don't have the values necessary to sustain their talent on a framework of character?

To me, the soul is your authentic self. It's who you are at your deepest point. I love Emerson's saying, "To be yourself in a world that is constantly trying to make you something else is the greatest accomplishment." Being yourself means feeding that authentic self, knowing who you are, and living consistently by what you say and what you do. Philosophically, you have to know your values. You have to have self-discovery. What do you *believe* in? "Inside each and every one of us," Junah says in *The Legend of Bagger Vance*, "is one authentic swing... something we was born with."

When I went to the University of Kansas, I learned quickly that I wasn't going to survive by being inauthentic. I couldn't run for money, I ran for my team and for the love of the sport. Bill Easton was a great coach, but in my opinion, he was focused on the material outcome: winning for the sake of winning. He wasn't focused on the growth of the athlete. It was a business, and I was there to do a job. I nearly lost my love of running—I nearly lost my swing—because it wasn't a holistic environment. I began the process of rediscovering it when I came back to Illinois and was surrounded by guys who didn't have athletic scholarships and who were running because they loved to run. This attitude offered me the opportunity to find my soul again.

Then I met Ted Haydon, and he was on the complete opposite end of the spectrum from Bill Easton. Ted's whole philosophy was centered on what he as a coach could do for the athlete. It was about the holistic development of the person and what you became as a result of the opportunity to be a part of his program. He didn't care about outcome. He never once said, "We have to win." What's the point of winning if you're not growing through the experience?

This philosophy saved me as a runner and influenced me as a coach. It goes much deeper than just running to win. It's something deep down in your soul that you're feeding with the joy of running. You're Running for Fun and Personal Bests!

Now I have been fighting a very serious cancer for the past few years. It is one reason why I have happily turned over the leadership of our cross country program to Coach Frank Grammarosso, my great coaching partner and friend. Life can become unstable. But through these trials, stability is regained not from things or resources but from the source of God reaching out his hand through the spirit of Jesus Christ. I am still assisting our runners and our track athletes, focusing on our invaluable culture, and sharing what I have learned over 50 years of coaching. I'm not giving up. And I'm embracing these words from the great college coach, Jimmy Valvano: "Cancer can take away all my physical abilities. It cannot touch my mind, it cannot touch my heart, and it cannot touch my soul. And those three things are going to carry on forever."

Whenever I am at my son Brent's home, my little grandson grabs my hand and says, "Pa Pa run!" and we move nonstop until something else catches his attention. He is a child at play, intrinsically enjoying the in-the-moment activity of running, which he enjoys and finds interesting and satisfying. Strange as it seems, this is the type of running we pursue at North Central.

External controlling forces, such as a parent or a coach, can try to impose obedience to a training regimen. But healthy, internal, self-generated motivations must surface in any performance activity when the rewards, incentives, and external forces are no longer present. External motivating pressures will work to a lesser extent initially but must become *intrinsic* to keep a runner motivated over the long haul.

Running is a natural activity. When a runner recognizes the challenge and satisfaction that comes from competing against himself (or herself), under the umbrella of freedom of choice, and takes a sense of ownership, surrounded by a supporting culture of coaches and teammates, he has the opportunity to experience the pure purpose of the activity, of the running itself, just like my grandson. He can enjoy the intrinsic satisfaction that comes from keeping the activity in perspective, having fun while experiencing personal bests. It becomes a part of his lifestyle.

The fun for our athletes includes the satisfaction that comes from absorbing the life lessons, the relationships, and the competition with themselves to see themselves getting better. The fun is striving to reach a personal best. The highest honor you can receive in our program isn't All-American. It's achieving a personal best. I don't care how fast someone is or what place he gets—the joy in his face when he realizes he's run faster or performed better than he ever has before is very difficult to put into meaningful words. But that's what it's all about here at North Central College. In a world that's becoming more materialistic, more professional, more outcome-oriented, we believe to the contrary that the ultimate competition is you against you, in the real "ah ha" moments in your life.

I remember having another one of those great "ah ha" moments shortly after my two young sons, Brent and Sam, were headed to the backyard one day to play baseball. Ah, the good old days! All kinds of personal feelings from my youth filled that moment for me: the smells, sounds, friends, and magic of fun playing baseball. "All right," I thought. My boys are calling on their own resources and creativity to play a game without a regulation field, umpires, uniforms, nine players on a side. Most important, there were no coaches or grownups directing their activity. They were *choosing* to play a sport for fun.

Sure, it is easy to romanticize the past, but as much as I can remember, that was the norm and the blueprint to my world when I was a kid—whether playing in the street, a farm pasture, or someone's side yard. Admittedly, those days are long gone, but although my memory gets clouded as I age, the outcome of those games was always clear to me—have fun just playing the game. Several years ago, I read an article in the newspaper that I couldn't really believe. The article was promoting a summer camp for kids to learn how to play. I was saddened to think that any youngster had to go to a camp to learn how to play.

I know, I know, it's a different world now. You can't go back. But the lessons and values learned along the way always help to shape who we are today. Needless to say, we are part of every experience and person we have met. As a coach, I have seen that these long-term values and an athlete's intrinsic goals have great effect on athletic competition. However, as a parent, I often worry about the overemphasis in our culture placed upon the outcome of winning rather than the process of playing, sometimes at the expense of a healthy perspective. Don't get me wrong, I am all for every competitive activity that helps an individual challenge themselves, or helps a team strive together, in the pursuit of excellence. But the drive to win should be about internal growth in the values of character regardless of winning or losing. The process will surely produce a winner and a loser, but the participants should not feel like losers as a result. You see, I believe strongly that, "You can win in losing and lose in winning."

By now many of you may be wondering where I am going with all this talk about my kids and baseball and winning in losing and losing in winning. Well, years ago I was at my son Sam's Major League Regional 10-year-old All-Star Tournament when I again saw the wisdom in this thought and realized what really counts in sports. Naperville, Sam's team, was leading in the bottom of the fifth inning. (Six innings comprise a complete game at that level.) The bases were loaded with two outs and Clarendon Hills was up to bat. The ball was grounded to Naperville's second baseman, who could have made the third out. As fate would have it, the ball bounced past him into center field, and Clarendon Hills scored the two tying runs. The game remained tied through the bottom of the sixth, thus sending it into extra innings.

While sitting there watching the game go into the bottom of the seventh tied, all I could think about was the second baseman. I was hoping he could get that missed ground ball out of his head. I was guessing that he felt the same way too. Ultimately, with a man on first and two outs, a ball was hit to Naperville's shortstop. He turned, ready to throw to second base to force the runner for the third out. But there was no one there to cover second base. Consequently, the shortstop's throw to first was too late. Clearly, the second baseman's focus was still on the play in the bottom of the fifth inning. Clarendon Hills went on to score the winning run, resulting in the elimination of the Naperville team from the regional championship after being handed its second loss of the tournament.

The Naperville team and the coach may have lost the game, but they didn't fail. As far as I am concerned, the team got outscored, but through the coach's positive influence, they won in losing on that day. Naperville Coach Mike Smith gave a speech to the team and the parents after the game about persistence and the values learned in the process of the season and the game. He acknowledged the team's disappointment, but reinforced the shared fun the boys had experienced through the process all through the season. It was a speech I will never forget or ever fail to appreciate. You see, that second baseman was my son, Sam. Coach Smith's uplifting tone and positive choice of post-game words put the lost game, and the tournament, in perspective. As a result, any focus on the second baseman was deflected.

Now don't get me wrong: a coach's goal is to win, as it should be. But the fact of the matter is 50% of the teams lose in every game played. In those situations, being a role model in how to "win in losing" demands your best and provides life lessons for everyone, and especially young athletes. Disappointment is a part of the sports experience. Albert Einstein once said, "Not everything that counts can be counted and not everything that can be counted counts."

When it really gets down to it, what really counts here: the sport or the individual?

To further support the point, let me give a contrasting example. Some time ago, Deer Creek grade school—coached by my brother, Jim—was playing Tremont in a basketball game. Keep in mind that these are two very small schools in small towns in central Illinois, and that I am also referring to grade school. Tremont was by far the superior team with talent led by a future professional football star. Clearly, the outcome was never going to be in question from the very start of the game. The final score was Tremont with over 100 points to Deer Creek's eight points. It was both curious and significant throughout the entire game: the Tremont coach kept his star player on the court the entire game to allow him to set an individual school scoring record.

Why do I use this troubling example? Well, victory should never be at the expense of the self-worth of oneself or of one's opponent. Individual growth should be the measure of winning, not the score or statistics. That's what I mean when I say, "You can win in losing and lose in winning."

I personally had one of these moments of "winning while losing" while flying home from the National AAU Track and Field Championship in California one year. It too had a dramatic impact on my life and my coaching. My mentor and UCTC coach, Ted Haydon, was once again involved. At the time, I was the lone runner for UCTC, Coach and I had just flown all the way to California, and I had just run a very disappointing race. You can imagine how down I was, especially since Ted had taken the time and the expense to accompany me across the country for my race.

Fortunately for me, the most remarkable trait about Coach Haydon was his ever-present sense of perspective that he managed to maintain for his athletes in the midst of any situation, however difficult. As always, he managed to say just the right things to me after my race. His timing for encouragement was uncanny. From all I can tell you, Ted did not need to accompany me to my meet, but he did. And after the race, he shared the wisdom that he felt was the most important role in coaching: "You have to be there for your athletes when things didn't go well. Everyone will be there in victories."

What a coach! What perspective. And what an example he set for me as a young coach. It's so clear to me now that athletes and people need their coaches and friends most during life's challenges. Some might say that Ted Haydon's motto was eerily similar that of my son's coach, Mike Smith: "Ask not what you can do for the sport. Ask how the sport can benefit the athlete."

Ideally, sport is not about *being* the best but rather about *doing* the best that you can within the boundaries and realities of your life. Balance is the key. For some today, over-organized sports and specialization too early in an athlete's life have become far too stressful. I have the notion that overspecialization and excessive focus on winning can zap the fun from many participants. Furthermore, athletes who overanalyze their performances or perform with unrealistic expectations inhibit their own creativity, stifle their long-term enjoyment, and eventually and ironically, may impede their own success. Again, our red line leading from our team locker room is an important reminder for our athletes to pursue balance in running—and in life.

Make no mistake; you cannot go back, and I am not suggesting it. But we as coaches can focus our athletes' attentions and efforts toward the right goals, as Coach Ted Haydon always did for his athletes. You see, I grew up in a time when stabilizing one's body happened naturally. Balance came from walking a street curb or a rail on the train tracks. Playing kick the can or even sometimes just kicking a rock down the sidewalk was common play. Upper body strength was developed by climbing trees. Speed was a by–product of tag rather than speed camps. Rules for games were made up *by the kids* and played with as many kids of any age or size as showed up on any given day, regardless of numbers or talent. Kids went from one season to the next, and played one sport at a time. Multiple-sport participation was commonplace and encouraged. There was never a political agenda associated with any of them.

The satisfaction in playing a sport didn't come from the outside with trophies but rather from the elation inside of just *playing*. As you can see, when I was a kid it never occurred to us to keep statistics or records. We played each sport, each game, for the pure intrinsic joy of the competitive feeling within the contest with our friends and teammates on any venue available.

These memories are probably an indication of my advanced years, but they are still vivid in my mind and influence me to encourage and instill in those I teach and coach the ideas I discovered along the way. I know what I have learned through my experimentation over the years, and realize as a father of five children the huge responsibility that I have for any student in my classroom and any athlete on our team: to help them grow and stand strong in the midst of life's challenges and difficulties. This is why I believe strongly that Dr. Jeff Duke's "Three Levels of

Coaching" should be holistically taught and coached within educational athletic programs today.

From childhood to college, playing a sport should be something we choose to do with no other reward than the opportunity to define winning by personal improvement physically, mentally, and spiritually. If other wonderful rewards, like scholarships, are earned, that's just icing on the cake of the personal rewards from *playing* sports. Sports are just one component in life's great experiences and not a whole life in itself. Sport at its best should not just be focused on "of the physical" but rather "through the physical," leading to lasting internal rewards. Run—compete, perform, work—for fun, and for personal bests. You'll be amazed at what you can achieve!

When I see all my athletes, regardless of talent, strength, or speed, take this and other lessons to heart and grow to become "Champions in the sport of life," I remember fully why I became a coach, and hope that God, my parents, and Ted Haydon are looking down on me proudly. I close this book, so long in the making, with the last four words spoken by Coach Normal Dale in the movie, *Hoosiers.* "I love you guys!"

Appendix I—North Central College Cross Country and Track & Field All-Americans

---

1964-65 All-American
Ron Trapp

1968-69 All-Americans
Bill Bradna
Bob Gray (2x AA)

1969-70 All-American
Mel Kinlow

1972-73 All-American
Glenn Behnke

1973-74 All-American
Scott Barrett
Glenn Behnke (NC & 2x AA)
National Champion (1)

1974-75 All-Americans
Scott Barrett (NC & 3x AA)
National Champion (2)
Steve Breunig
Joe Clendenny (2x AA)
Jeff Garmon
Ron Hankel
Eddie McGee
Kevin Markwell

1975-76 All-Americans
Bruce Fischer
Scott Gyssler
Jim Mitchell
Jerry Hendron

1976-77 All-Americans
Dave Bashaw
Bruce Fischer (2x AA)
Jim Mitchell
Ron Piro

1977-78 All-Americans
Bruce Fischer
Jim Martin
Don Milkent (2x AA)
Jeff Milliman
Mike Mores
Wayne Reynolds
Robert Simmert

1978-79 All-Americans
Bruce Fischer
Rich Behlmer
Steve Jawor (2x AA)
Tom Kerwin
Joe Mallon
Don Milkent
Jeff Milliman
Jim Nichols
Dan Skarda

1979-80: 7 All-Americans
Steve Jawor
Tom Kerwin (NC & 1x AA)
National Champion (3)
John Linder
Jeff Milliman (2x AA)
Dan Skarda (2x AA)

1980-81 All-Americans
John Linder (2x AA)
Jim Martin
Jeff Milliman (2x NC & 3x AA)
National Champion (4, 5)
Tim O'Grady
Jay Rogers
Dan Siewert (3x AA)
Jay Wesley
Pat Youngs

1981-82 All-Americans
Tony Bleull
Bob Dunphey
Ray Krauss
Bill O'Neill
Dan Siewert (2x AA)

1982-83 All-Americans
Tony Bleull (2x AA)
Bob Dunphey (2x AA)
Ray Krauss
Matt Nolan
Jay Rogers

1983-84 All-Americans

Tony Bleull (NC & 1x AA)
National Champon (6)
Bob Dunphey
Ray Krauss
Kevin Mercer

1984-85 All-Americans

Bob Dunphey
Joe Gross
Jim Jones
Matt Nolan
Larry Wood

1985-86 All-Americans

Gary Peterson (3x AA)
Kurt Hasenstein
Brian Lamb
Larry Wood

1986-87 All-Americans

Dan Baker
Pete Bartelson
Joel Bowman
Marc Browning
Kurt Hasenstein
Jim Jones
Terrance Jordan
Brian Lamb
Gary Peterson
Dennis Piron (2x AA)
Joe Plutz
Jim VanHootegem

1987-88 All-Americans

Mark Bachtold
Dan Baker (NC & 2x AA)
National Champion (7)
Joel Bowman
John Collett (2x AA)
Dana Epperson (2x AA)
Tim Foley
Doug Hearn
Jay Jackson
Brian Lamb (3x AA)
Joe Plutz (2x AA)
Rich Scopp (2x AA)
Brad Todden
Jim VanHootegem (2x AA)
Shawn Welti (NC & 2x AA)
National Champion (8)

1988-89 All-Americans

Ron Arb
Dan Baker (1x NC & 4x AA)
National Champion (9)
Pete Bartelson
Joel Bowman (2x AA)
Jan Cado (4x NC & 5x AA)
National Champion (10, 11, 12, 13)
John Collet (3x AA)
Doug Hearn
Brian Lamb (2x AA)
Phil Malone
Harold McCadd
Joe Plutz (2x AA)

Rich Scopp (1x NC & 3x AA)
National Champion (14)
Brad Todden
Bill Toland (2x AA)
Jim VanHootegem (2x AA)
Shawn Welti (3x AA)

1989-90 All-Americans

Pete Bartelson
Derron Bishop
Jan Cado (3x NC & 6x AA)
National Champion (15, 16, 17)
Dave Columbus
Tim Johnson
Scott King
Harold McCadd
Gerald McCadd
Wendel McRaven
Jim VanHootegem (2x AA)
Shawn Welti (2x AA)
Brian Wilson (2x AA)

1990-91 All-Americans

Joe Baker (2x AA)
Derron Bishop (3x AA)
Anthony Brent
Bob Cisler (2x AA)
Andre Coleman (2x AA)
Jon Koval
Gerald McCadd (2x AA)
Harold McCadd (2x AA)
Britton Roth
Dan Snyder

Gale VanRossem
Brian Wilson

1991-92 All-Americans

Joe Baker (2x AA)
Derron Bishop (2x AA)
Andre Coleman
David Jones
Jon Koval
Dan Mayer (3x AA)
Gerald McCadd
Harold McCadd
Dan Rowan (2x AA)
Gale Van Rossem
Steve White

1992-93 All-Americans

Derron Bishop (2x AA)
Andre Coleman (4x AA)
Rob Harvey
David Jones (2x AA)
Dan Mayer (2x NC & 4x AA)
National Champion (18, 19)
Ed Rhyne (2x AA)
Gale VanRossem (2x AA)
Steve White
Dave Zimmerman (2x AA)

1993-94 All-Americans

Joel Badie
Nate Breed
Matt Brill (2x AA)
Mike Brindley (2x AA)

Andre Coleman (3x AA)

Jim Dickerson (3x AA)

Brian Fennelly (1x NC & 2x AA)
National Champion (20)

Brian Henz (2x AA)

Dan Iverson

Brian Johnson (2x AA)

David Jones (2x AA)

Dan Mayer (4x NC & 4x AA)
National Champion (21, 22, 23, 24)

Justin Tabour

John Weigel (3x AA)

1994-95 All-Americans

Matt Brill (2x AA)

Jims Dickerson (3x AA)

Brian Henz (3x AA)

Brian Johnson

Justin Tabour

John Weigel (1x NC & 4x AA)
National Champion (25)

Rafeal Willams

1995-96 All-Americans

Ryan Board

Matt Brill (4x AA)

Erik Diekman

Luther Olson

Vince Reh

Nate Riley

Jeff Stiles

John Weigel (1x NC & 4x AA)
National Champion (26)

1996-97 All-Americans

Nate Breed

Matt Brill (1x NC & 1x AA)
National Champion (27)

Jack Kafel

Emil Ostberg

Tony Rizzo (3x AA)

Jeff Stiles

Cam Stuber

Erik Diekman

David Thompson (1x NC & 3x AA) *National Champion (28)*

Mike Wichmann

Joel Williams (2x AA)

1997-98 All-Americans

Ryan Board (2x AA)

Matt Brill (1x AA)

Zach Bukal (1x NC & 1x AA)
National Champion (29)

Erik Diekman

Steve Draminski

Emil Ostberg (1x NC & 1x AA)
National Champion (30)

Tony Rizzo (2x AA)

Jeff Stiles (4x AA)

Will Swain

David Thompson (2x NC & 4x AA)
National Champion (32, 33)

Joel Williams (1x NC & 1x AA)
National Champion (34)

DuWayne Wright

Colin Young

1998-99 All-Americans
Zach Bukal

Jon Coleman

Erik Diekman (1x NC & 1x AA)
National Champion (35)

Ryan Jordan

Tim McCoskey (2x AA)

Matt Moran

Tony Rizzo

DuWayne Wright

Colin Young

1999-2000 All-Americans
Jeremy Borling

Zach Bukal (1x NC & 1x AA)
National Champion (36)

Charlie Califf (1x NC & 4x AA)
National Champion (37)

Jeff Hansen

Ryan Kane

Tim McCoskey (3x NC & 5x AA)
National Champion (38, 39, 40)

Adam Moodie

Justin Rapp

Ed Reigert (1x NC & 4x AA)
National Champion (41)

Jason Tracy

Colin Young (1x NC & 4x AA)
National Champion (42)

2000-01 All-Americans
Jeremy Borling

James Houston

Tim McCoskey (1x NC & 1x AA)
National Champion (43)

Justin Rapp (2x AA)

2001-02 All-Americans
Paul Crumrine

Brian DeLoriea

Mark Hawkinson

James Houston (2x AA)

Paul Kenost

Jane King

Adam Moodie

Tim Nelson

Justin Rapp (1x NC & 2x AA)
National Champion (44)

Pat Rizzo

Tony Rizzo (3x AA)

Kyle Stumpenhorst

2002-03 All-Americans
Brian DeLoriea (2x AA)

Andy Enright

Phillip Gorrill

Tim Nelson

Brandon Strode

Greg Targosz (2x AA)

2003-04 All-Americans
Paul Crumrine

Brian DeLoriea (2x AA)

Nick Hird

Andy Hubner

Pat Rizzo (2x AA)

Dan Rodriguez
Brandon Strode
Kyle Stumpenhorst (2x AA)

2004-05 All-Americans
Omar Abdullah
Jacob Bremer
Brian DeLoriea (1x NC & 2x AA)
National Champion (45)
Roland Hopkins
Andy Hubner (2x AA)
Dave Johnson
Ryan Kwiek
Greg Memmesheimer (2x AA)
Adam Pennington (2x AA)
Pat Rizzo (3x AA)
Dan Rodriguez
Kyle Stumpenhorst (2x AA)
Julius White (2x AA)

2005-06 All-Americans
Michael Bina
Chris Bosworth
Nick Hird
Andy Hubner
David Johnson
Ryan Kwiek
Adam Pennington (3x AA)
Pat Rizzo
Steven Schnackel
Julius White (2x AA)

2006-07 All-Americans
Nick Hird
Greg Jackson
David Johnson
Adam Pennington (2x AA)
Julius White

2007-08 All-Americans
Michael Bina
Jon Howard
Greg Jackson
Adam Johnson
Justin McQuality
Adam Pennington (3x AA)
Jake Winder

2008-09 All-Americans
Kyle Brady (3x AA)
Nate Hird
Michael Spain (3x AA)
Jake Winder (1x NC & 1x AA)
National Champion (46)
John Wood

2009-10 All-Americans
Jacob Austin
Dan Benton (1x NC & 2x AA)
National Champion (47)
Matt Borchardt (2x AA)
Kyle Brady (2x NC & 4x AA)
National Champion (48, 49)
Sean Carlson
Jon Caron (1x NC & 1x AA)
National Champion (50)

269

Ryan Carrigan

Peter Geraghty

Dayton Henriksen (1x NC & 1x AA)
National Champion (51)

Nate Hird

Jon Howard (1x NC & 1x AA)
National Champion (52)

Neal Klein

Nathan Rutz

Michael Spain (3x AA)

Thomas Stacey (2x AA)

Steven Stack

Jake Winder (2x NC & 2x AA)
National Champion (53, 54)

John Wood (2x AA)

2010-11 All-Americans

Dan Benton (1x NC & 3x AA)
National Champion (55)

Jon Caron

Randal Ellison

Peter Geraghty (1x NC & 2x AA)
National Champion (56)

Zach Heerspink

Jon Howard (2x AA)

Robert Kaputska

Dan Kerley

Neal Klein

Matt Perez

Michael Spain (3x NC & 4x AA)
National Champion (57, 58, 59, 60)

Thomas Stacey

Nathan Warstler

Josh Winder (2x AA)

John Wood

2011-12 All-Americans

Dan Benton (2x NC & 2x AA)
National Champion (61, 62)

Jon Caron

John Crain

Peter Geraghty (1x NC & 1x AA)
National Champion (63)

Dionte Hackler (1x NC and 3x AA)
National Champion (64)

Marlen Hamilton

Zach Heerspink

Tim Hird

Jon Howard

Bai Kabba (1x NC & 2x AA)
National Champion (65)

Dan Kerley

Neal Klein

Juliano Lodi

Mustapha Olaoye (1x NC & 1x AA)
National Champion (66)

Matt Perez

Thomas Stacey

Josh Winder (1x NC & 2x AA)
National Champion (67)

John Wood (2x AA)

2012-13 All-Americans

John Crain (1x NC & 4x AA)
National Champion (68)

Pat Foley

Marlen Hamilton

Zach Heerspink

Dan Kerley

Juliano Lodi

Matt Muth

Abraham Oshipitan

Josh Winder (1x NC & 2x AA)
National Champion (69)

2013-14 All-Americans

John Crain (3x NC & 5x AA)
National Champion (70, 71, 72)

Dionte Hackler

Tim Hird

Troy Kelleher (2x AA)

Zach Kirby

Roger Klein (2x AA)

Travis Morrison

Matt Muth

Derek Nelson (2x AA)

Mustapa Olaoye

Richard Ruske

Adam Weidner

2014-15 All-Americans

Ben Dickshinski

Travis Morrison (1x NC & 4x AA)
National Champion (73)

Matt Muth

Derek Nelson

Ryan Root

Richard Ruske

Aron Sebhat (3x AA)

Luke Winder (2x NC & 2x AA)
National Champion (74, 75)

2015-16 All-Americans

Zach Kirby (2x AA)

Ben Nordman (2x AA)

Peyton Piron (2x AA)

Zach Plank (3x AA)

Aron Sebhat (2x AA)

Daniel Spaccapanicca (2x AA)

Tim Vazquez

Luke Winder (2x NC & 2x AA)
National Champion (76, 77)

2016-17 All-Americans

Ethan Adlifinger (2x AA)

Al Baldonado

Chris Buechner

Zach Hird (2x AA)

Zach Kirby

Dylan Kuipers

Spencer LaHaye

Josh Martin

Ben Nordman

Dhruvil Patel (3x AA)

Peyton Piron (2x AA)

Zach Plank

Adam Poklop

Daniel Spaccapanicca

Luke Winder (2x NC & 2x AA)
National Champion (78)

2017-18 All-Americans

Michael Anderson

Al Baldonado

Jared Borowsky

Chris Buechner

Maceo Findlay

Zach Hird

Dylan Kuipers (2x AA)

Kyle LeBlanc

Ben Nordman (2x AA)

Matt Norvell (2x AA)

Dan O'Keefe

Dhruvil Patel (3x NC & 5x AA)
National Champion (79, 80, 81)

Peyton Piron (4x AA)

Dan Spaccapaniccia (2x AA)

Michael Stanley (2x AA)

Luke Winder(1x NC & 1x AA)
National Champion (82)

2018-19 All-Americans

Al Baldonado

Chris Buechner

Zach Hird

Matt Osmulski

Dhruvil Patel (3x NC & 3x AA)
National Champion (83, 84, 85)

2019-20 All-Americans

Nick Licari

Gabe Pommier

Matt Osmulski

2020-21 All-Americans

Nick Janca (2x AA)

Gabe Pommier (1x NC & 3x AA)—
National Champion (86)

Michael Stanley (1x NC & 1x AA)—
National Champion (87)

751 Total All-Americans
87 Total National Champions

Updated: 8/6/21

Appendix II—Coaches, Volunteers, Supporters

Here is a list—sadly incomplete—of the many men and women who have helped me coach our North Central teams over more than 55 years. In no way could I, or our program, have had the success we have had without the help and guidance of these wonderful coaches and former NCC athletes.

Marv Meinz	Paul Crumrine
Hank Guenther	Tony Daniels
George Cyr	Sean Denard
Lloyd Krumlauf	Jim Dickerson
Glenn Behnke	Kevin Downs
Jeff Heller	Gary Englehorn
Ken Popejoy	Tommy Ferguson
Frank Gramarosso	Pat Gora
Jerry Allanach	Pat Gray
Dave Bashaw	Dimetri Gueroguiev
Dan Benton	Scott Gyssler
Mike Bina	Kurt Hasenstein
Matt Borchardt	Pat Heenan
Marc Browning	Ken Helberg
Kyle Brady	Brian Henz
Larry Brown	Nick Hird
Pat Carney	Tim Hird
John Collet	Zach Hird
Mike Considine	Greg Huffaker
Tim Crawford	Brian Johnson

Dan Johnson

Walter Johnson

Dale Koepnick

Ray Krauss

Jordan Kremer

Mike Luchessi

Sean Magnuson

Doug Malinsky

Vern Martin

Yonny Mascote

Don Milkent

Tom Minser

Mahesh Narayanan

Derrik Nelson

Jim Nichols

Jamie Norton

Tim O'Grady

Dan O'Keefe

Mike Perez

Todd Radeky

Kevin Rafferty

Paul Rewerts

Ed Riegert

Tom Roderick

Dan Savage

Rich Scott

Bob Schrader

Tyler Sheehan

Joe Silich

Eric Simon

Matt Sinnott

Lee Slick

Matt Souvannasing

Jim Spivey

Jeff Stiles

Mike Stull

Gerry Stormer

Justin Tabour

David Thompson

Jake Till

Brad Todden

Phil Van Leer

Jim Wachenheim

Ed Wallace

Brian Walsh

John Weigel

Steve Weisbrook

Chris Wheaton

Hannah Weiss

Tom Whittaker

Joel Williams

Jake Winder

Josh Winder

Luke Winder

Tim Winder

Bob Winslow

Nathan Worstler

Tyler Yunk

Keith Zobrist

Here again is a partial list—I can no longer remember them all—of the hundreds of volunteers and supporters of our NCAA Division III North Central athletics programs over 55 years. Many many names have been forgotten and left off this list. But these generous volunteers represent the others, all of whom helped to make our program so fun and so successful. Without them and their generosity, our track & field and cross country programs could not have been so successful and, in fact, would not have been possible..

Coach Ted Hayden—Role Model
Arlo Schilling, NCC President
Gail Swing, NCC President
Hal Wilde, NCC President
Troy Hammond, NCC President
Larry & Charmaine Gregory—Benefactors
Don Wehrli—Benefactor
Reverend Don Borling—Spiritual Coach
Wayne Reynolds—Alumni Minister
Keith Douglas—Alumni Minister
Dave Klusendorf—Alumni Official
Irv Keehler—Benefactor
Russ Poole—Faculty Rep & Supporter
Eric Thornton—Alumni Official
Gary Barrett—Alumni Official
Joe Hartmann—Team Doctor
Don Deetjen—Alumni Benefactor
Sheldon Hayer—Friend & Official
Paul & Jackie Rewerts—Alumni Supporters
Bob & Linda Schrader—Alumni Supporters

Tom Brunick—Friend & Supporter
Keith Jacobi—Friend & Official
Greg Klebe—Alumni Official
Pat Heenan—Alumni Official
Beth Grys—Alumni Official
Jim Rice—Friend Official
Scott & Kelly McCleary—Friends & Supporters

Appendix III—NCC Alumni who Became Coaches

NCC Cross Country and Track & Field Alumni who became Coaches at other Colleges and Schools— Current or Former Schools

Mike Adamson—Plainfield East High School (HS)
Ethan Adlfinger—North Central College (NCC)
Jeff Allen
Ryan Armstrong
Dave Ashton—Naperville Central HS
Jake Austin
Al Baldanado
Ron Barnes—Peru St. Bede HS
Ryan Bartel
Dave Bashaw—North Central College
John Beehler
Jason Beer
Glenn Behnke—North Central College
Dan Benton—North Central College
Mike Bina—North Central College
Matt Borchardt—North Central College
Chris Bosworth—Lake Park HS
Bill Bradna
Kyle Brady—North Central College
Jeff Bral—Bartlett HS
Eric Brechtel—Naperville Central HS
Jake Bremer
Matt Brinkmier

Tim Brodeur
Clem Brown—Naperville IL
Marc Browning—North Central College
Chris Buechner
Greg Burks—Hinkley-Big Rock HS
Dan Buys
Rick Cadena
Jan Cado—Personal Trainer/Advisor
Sean Carlson—Notre Dame University
Pat Carney—St. Charles East HS, NCC
Aaron Carper—Minnetonka HS (MN)
Jeff Chiapello—University of St. Francis (IL)
Joe Chiro—Lake Park HS
Bob Cora—Romeoville HS
Mikey Cobb
John Collet—North Central College
Mike Considine—College of DuPage (IL), NCC
John Crain
Tim Crawford—North Central College
Paul Crumrine—North Central College
Cambron Culpepper
George Cyr—Naperville Central HS, NCC
Tony Daniels—North Central College
Sean Denard—North Central College
Brian Dennison—Galesburg HS
Jim Dickerson—North Central College
Jim DiDomenico
Steve Draminiski—West Chicago HS
Ben Draper
Nick Drendel
Nick Dunn
Tim Ehlebracht
Brian Evans—Thornwood HS

Walt Farley—Sandwich IL
Bill Feind—Clarendon Hills Middle School (MS)
Brian Fennelly—Main South HS
Tommy Ferguson—North Central College
Bruce Fischer—Kaskaskia College
Stephen Fleagle
Tim Foley—Bolingbrook HS
Todd Fonck
John Fulton—Chicago IL
Mike Garcia—Springfield Lanphier HS
Mitch Gilbert
Shane Gillispie—East Aurora HS
Weert Goldenstein—Streamwood HS
Ted Golota
Bob Gray—Eugene OR
Patrick Griffin—Trinity Academy (WI)
Gary Groharing—Naperville Lincoln Junior High
Stan Gruska
Scott Gyssler—North Central College
Chase Hall
Ron Hankel
Kevin Harrington—St. Charles North HS
Travis Hartke—Iowa State University
Rob Harvey—Wheaton-Warrenville South HS
Kurt Hasenstein—Glenbrook South HS, NCC
Doug Hearn
Pat Heenan—North Central College
Mark Hedrick—Geneva HS
Don Helberg—Wheaton North HS
Jeff Helberg
Ken Helberg—Wheaton-Warrenville South HS, NCC
Jeff Heller—North Central College
Brian Henz—North Central College

Chad Hillman—Batavia HS
Nick Hird—North Central College
Tim Hird—North Central College
Zach Hird—North Central College
Chuck Hoff
Mark Holt
Guthrie Hood—Tolono Unity Junior High
Roland Hopkins
Kevin Horst
James Houston—Plainfield South HS
Curtis Hudson
Greg Huffaker—Illinois Wesleyan University, NCC
Nick Hurd
Steve Imig—St. Charles North HS
Dan Iverson—Naperville North HS
Greg Jackson
Jay Jackson
Brian Johnson—North Central College
Dan Johnson—St. Anne HS, NCC
Walter Johnson—North Central College, A.D.
Bai Kabba
Bobby Kallien
Ryan Kane
Kerry Kelley—East Aurora HS
Nate Kennedy—Bolingbrook HS
Roger Klein
Dave Klussendorf—Naperville Kennedy Junior High
Ron Koch—O'Fallon HS
Dale Koepnick—Coal City HS, NCC
Mike Kopczyk
Jon Koval—Peoria Woodruff HS
Ray Krauss—North Central College
Jordan Kremer—North Central College

Jeff Krumlauf
Lloyd Krumlauf—North Central College
Bob Lewis—Downers Grove North HS
Nick Licari
Kevin Licht
Matthew Littleton—Virginia Wesleyan College
Brian Long
Dan Lowry
Mike Lucchesi—North Central College
Jim Macnider—Schaumburg HS & Harper CC
Jon Macnider—Schaumburg HS
Kirk Macnider—Hoffman Estates & Schaumburg HS
Joe Mallon—Chicago St. Ignatius
Brendan Mariano—Schaumburg HS
Kevin Markwell—Plainfield HS
Vern Martin
Jeff Martinez
Yonny Mascote—North Central College
Zion Mason
Tim McCoskey—Neuqua Valley HS
Wendell McCraven—Texas A&M University
Eddie McGee
Nolan McKenna
Robell McMiller—Chicago De La Salle HS
Justin McQuality
Tyler McQuality
Greg Memmesheimer
Kip Mihalek
Don Milkent—North Central College
Fred Miller—Oswego HS
Tom Minser—North Central College
Matt Moran—Chicago Reavis HS
Don Moravec—Downers Grove North HS

Mike Mores—Wheaton-Warrenville South HS
Bob Murray
Matt Muth
Luke Nally
Mahesh Narayanan—North Central College
Derek Nelson
Scott Nelson—Wheaton St. Francis HS
Dan Newkirk—Litchfield HS
Jim Nichols—Ithaca College (NY), NCC
Matt Nolan—Livermore, CA
Jacob Norman—Delevan HS (WI)
Josh Norman—Pekin HS
Jamie Norton—North Central College
Mike Norwood
Tim O'Grady—Lancaster Catholic HS (PA), NCC
Dan O'Keefe—North Central College
John Oliver
Matt Osmulski
Chris Pelz
Matt Perez
Mike Perez—North Central College
Mike Pierce
Ron Piro—Wheaton North HS
Dennis Piron—Batavia HS
John Prieboy
Jim Probst
Todd Radecky—North Central College
Kevin Rafferty—Waubonsie Valley HS, NCC
Justin Rapp—Eastern Michigan University
Jerome Reed—Chicago Prosser HS
Vince Reh—Lincoln-Way HS
Ed Reigert—North Central College
Andy Remley

Paul Rewerts—Downers Grove South HS
Wayne Reynolds—Boys Town, NE
Chris Rhode—Nequa Valley HS
Greg Riordan
Pat Rizzo
Tony Rizzo—West Aurora HS
Byron Robertson
Jason Rogers
Jay Rogers—Glenwood HS
Ryan Root
Mark Ruff
Emilio Saraga
Dan Savage
"Big Daddy" Bob Schrader—Naperville Lincoln JH
Kevin Schnable
Rich Scott—North Central College
Dave Shafron—Niles North HS
Tyler Sheehan—North Central College
Ken Shaw—Somonauk HS
Larry Simmert—Rockford Christian HS
Eric Simon—Oswego HS, NCC
Matt Sinnott—West Aurora HS, NCC
Lee Slick—North Central College
Craig Snyder—Tiffin Columbian HS (OH)
Matt Souvannasing—North Central College
Mike Spain
Aaron Spivey
Steve Stack
Geoff Steinbeck—Arrowhead HS (WI)
Chris Stelzer—Gonzaga University (WA)
Jeff Stiles—Washington University of St. Louis
Mike Stull—North Central College
Will Swain

Gerry Stormer—North Central College
Josh Stumpenhorst—Naperville Central HS
Kevin Swann
Justin Tabor—North Central College
David Thompson—University of Dubuque (IA), NCC
Eric Thornton—Naperville North HS
Jake Till—North Central College
Brad Todden
Tayler Throckmorton—North Central College
Mike Vandeleur—Neuqua Valley HS
Jim VanHootegem—Texas A&M University
Phil VanLear—Chicago St. Ignatius HS, NCC
Ed Victor—Washington High School
Jim Wachenheim—University of Miami (OH), NCC
Andy Walsh
Brian Walsh—North Central College
Jeff Weigel
John Weigel—Naperville Kennedy Junior High, NCC
Steve Weisbrook—Naperville Central HS, NCC
Hannah Weiss—North Central College
Shawn Welti—Middleton HS (WI)
Chris Wheaton—Batavia HS, NCC
Tom Whitaker—North Central College
Steve White—Robbinsale Armstrong HS (MN)
Aaron White—Elgin HS
Joel Williams—North Central College
Ray Williams—Grand Valley State University (MI)
Brian Wilson—Detroit Catholic Central (MI)
Jake Winder—North Central College
Josh Winder—North Central College
Luke Winder—North Central College
Bob Wislow—North Central College
Steve Witte—Kewanee HS

Pete Wolf—Westmont HS
Ronnie Woods—Cairo HS
Ben Wordman
Nathan Worstler—North Central College
John Wood
Colin Young
Tyler Yunk—North Central College
Jeff Zematis—Vernon Hills HS
Keith Zobrist—North Central College
Jerry Zoephel

Sadly, this list of my former athletes who became coaches themselves is incomplete. My apologies to anyone I have forgotten. The school names listed here may not be up-to-date, as sometimes our alumni are hired away to help a new school or college and we don't always get our records updated properly. The high school programs listed here are in Illinois, unless otherwise marked.

Many many of these athletes have volunteered to help us here at North Central either before or after their coaching careers at other schools. We would not have had the robust and successful program we have had for 50-plus years without the help of these great alumni.

I'm so proud to have had so many young men and women pass through our North Central College athletic program and go on to spread our message of "Run for Fun and Personal Bests" to other high school and college programs. I pray that I have set a good example for them for how to be a coach and a guide to the young people who are entrusted to their care.

—Coach Al Carius

Acknowledgements

Thank you for making the commitment of time and patience to read through the pages of my book. The words and thoughts for this labor of love have come from *every* person who I have met and *every* experience that I have encountered over the course of my life. Any wisdom I share, I attribute to and dedicate to my gifts of faith, my family, my friends, and countless others who have touched my life. The words and thoughts for this labor of love have come from these sources.

I am certain that numerous names and personal interactions have not been specifically referenced herein. I deeply apologize to those whose names and stories are missing. I regret any deserving recognition omitted in the lists of our wonderful coaches, athletes, volunteers, and other contributors to our rich and storied history of North Central College Cross Country and Track & Field. We are the program we are, and I am who I am, because of each of you who have blessed my life. Each of you are a part of my life's mission, and for that I am eternally grateful. My heart swells with the thought of every one of you.

Faith, family, and friends! Having a solid spiritual foundation provides the base to build a life. My belief in God and his Son Jesus Christ is my framework for the essential values of my very being. My parents, my brother Jim, and my sister Marjorie added life, love, and great wisdom to every day of my youth. They created my true core and foundation while

I was growing up. For their moral guidance, love, and companionship, I thank them every day. My athletes, if they have benefited over the years from my guidance and my example, have my parents and my siblings to thank.

How can I begin to thank my wife Pam and my children—the five treasures of my life—Scott, Rick, Stephanie, Brent, and Sam, for all their love and support? They and their families have given me the inspiration and the reason to be who and what I am as a man, a father, and a mentor. They all have a deep understanding of what one gives up when one's husband and father is a college coach. Pam and my children have given me time and great patience to allow me to fulfill my life's path as a coach. Pam has been the glue holding our family together during all my time away while coaching. To all of you, I am truly grateful, and know that with you I have been blessed.

We all need a team as we go through life and my life's teammates have been fantastic! One doesn't hold any position for more than 50 years without the love and assistance of thousands of friends and colleagues. Leading that long list, of course, is Coach Ted Haydon of the University of Chicago Track Club. Without Ted's influence, example, and values, I couldn't have become the coach I became.

Our hundreds of assistant coaches at North Central over the years, such as Glenn Behnke, Jim Nichols, Jim Wachenheim, Ken Popejoy, and Frank Gramarosso—all great runners and inspiring coaches—helped create a philosophically successful culture for our student athletes. All of our coaches—dozens more are listed at the back of this book—have contributed to this positive atmosphere and great learning experience for our athletes.

Yet I must single out one representative coach and his lasting impact on our program. Coach Frank "Grammy"

Gramarosso, my great coaching partner and friend for the past 38 years, has had a dramatic impact on expanding the reach of our philosophy into a balanced and successful track & field program. North Central Track & Field and Cross Country would not have had its sustained success without Frank's dedication and guidance. I am delighted that Frank has accepted the baton hand off from me and is now heading our cross country and track & field programs into the future. He is an amazing coach, father, and leader, and assures the continued success of and a bright future for our North Central program.

North Central College has been a "Special Kind of Place" where our athletes can get a "holistic" education while exercising their intrinsic passion to compete. Our program has been blessed by the involvement and assistance of "special people" as well. We have had countless caring faculty-athletic liaisons like Russ Poel and Marv Meinz, generous community boosters like Larry Gregory, Dick Wehrli, and Don Deetjen, and athletic and college advocates like Hank Guenther, Patrick Gray, Shirley Haines, and Jim Miller to name but a few. I also thank the very supportive Presidents of North Central College under whom I have served: Arlo Schilling, Gail Swing, Acting President Rich Luze, Hal Wilde, and Troy Hammond. They and the college have provided the platform for me to teach and coach, and have championed me and our programs for the past 56 years. They recognized the large and important part athletics plays in the total education of the students of North Central College.

I wish to thank all of our wonderful alumni for their moral support and their willingness to stay connected with our institutional mission after they began their lives outside the college. Their every visit, call, letter, text, or email gives me great energy and joy. As well, I want to say, "Thank You!" to the thousands of volunteers who have worked so hard to help us to host regular yearly competitions for our student athletes. The list of these volunteers would be endless, but special thanks for their life-long commitments go to Greg Klebe, the late Pat Heenan, David Klussendorf, Pat Gora, Jeff Heller, Lloyd Krumlauf, and the members of our Winged Foot Club.

Many friends have influenced the completion of this book, which for years has accumulated on bits and pieces of notepaper in a box as handwritten stories about our program's history. It never would have reached the form of a book without the help of people like Keith Zobrist, Pat Gora, Eric Thornton, Glenn Behnke, Don Borling, Dave Ferguson, Zach Hird, Eileen McBrien, John Weigel, Chris Wheaton, Laura Budler, Donn Behnke, Jeff Stiles, Colleen Carius, Matt Sinnott, Bob Dunphey, and Gerry Gems. Frank Martin copyedited the manuscript repeatedly, organized my key Culture chapter, and contributed his wonderful Forward.

I specifically express my heartfelt depth of appreciation to Dave Hartmann, one of the "No Names" from our first NCAA National Championship Team in 1975, for his insight and unique perspective on the bulk of my coaching career. Dave took all my notes, pieces of paper, thoughts, and conversations I shared with him, and organized, clarified, edited, and directed my efforts in writing this book. I could not have even pulled the pieces together without his help. Our discussions and shared ideas are an invaluable part of this finished product. Thank you, my lifelong friend.

And thank you, more broadly, to all of the members of my North Central College community—my life's teammates—who have embraced my philosophy and helped us build this wonderful team history together.

Made in the USA
Middletown, DE
20 July 2022

69539226R00179